The General Data Protection Regulation
in Plain Language

The General Data Protection Regulation in Plain Language

Bart van der Sloot

Amsterdam University Press

Cover illustration: Defense Advanced Research Project Agency (DARPA)

Cover design: Gijs Mathijs Ontwerpers
Lay-out: Crius Group, Hulshout

ISBN   978 94 6372 6511
e-ISBN   978 90 4854 466 0
NUR   740

Table of Contents

Who is who?

- *Europe* is a continent of about 50 officially recognised sovereign states.
- The *Council of Europe* is a European supra-national organisation of which most European countries – 47 in total – are members. The Council of Europe focuses almost exclusively on the protection of human rights.
- The *European Convention on Human Rights* is the main legal instrument of the Council of Europe, covering essential civil and political human rights, such as the right to a fair trial, the right to privacy, freedom of expression and the principle of non-discrimination.
- The *European Court of Human Rights* is the highest court of the Council of Europe and deals with the interpretation of the European Convention on Human Rights.
- The *European Union* is a supra-national organisation of which 28 European countries are members (27 after Brexit has been finalised). Originally, the European Union (EU) was mainly concerned with socio-economic issues and the creation of a single European market, but more recently it has also adopted legal instruments that concern the protection of fundamental rights.
- A *Member State* is the term used for a sovereign country that is a member of the European Union, such as France, Germany and Italy.
- The *European Commission* can be compared to the government (executive power) of the EU; each Member State can nominate one Commissioner (to be compared with a minister). The head of the European Commission is elected by the European Parliament. The Commission drafts most of the legislative proposals, although it is itself not formally part of the legislative power.
- The *European Parliament* is the parliament of the EU; its members are elected through EU-wide elections. Together

with the Council of the European Union, the Parliament forms the legislative power of the EU. It also controls and critically assesses the functioning of the EU's executive power.

- The *Council of the European Union* consists of the heads of state of each EU Member State. When legislative proposals by the Commission are discussed with the Parliament and the Council, this is typically called the trialogue.
- The European *Court of Justice* is the highest court in the European Union and deals with the interpretation of the Charter of Fundamental Rights, the General Data Protection Regulation and other legal instruments of the European Union.
- The *Charter of Fundamental Rights* can be compared to the constitution of the European Union, containing the fundamental rights and rules related to the organisation and functioning of the EU.
- The *General Data Protection Regulation* (GDPR) lays down the general data protection framework within the European Union. Adopted in 2016, it replaces its 1995 predecessor, the Data Protection Directive. The GDPR is applicable as of May 2018.
- Also adopted in 2016 and applicable as of May 2018, the *Law Enforcement Directive* provides the data protection framework for processing personal data in the law enforcement context. These rules are in essence similar to those of the GDPR, but allow for more exceptions when necessary in light of the fight against crime or the protection of public order.
- *Personal data* is information relating to an identified or identifiable natural person (meaning a person of flesh and blood and not, for example, a legal person). The sentence 'Chelsea Manning is a hero' contains personal data, the sentence 'Grass is green' or 'Amazon's delivery service stinks' does not.
- The *data subject* is the person that the personal data refer to. In the sentence 'Eric has blue eyes', Eric is the data subject.

- The GDPR applies when personal data are processed, where *processing* is almost every action involving personal data, such as gathering, storing and using, but also correcting, completing and deleting data.
- The *controller* is the person or organisation responsible for processing personal data. The controller decides which data will be processed, how and why. For example, if a pizza delivery service processes the name and the post code of a customer, the pizza delivery service is the controller.
- The controller can be assisted by a *processor*. The processor is the person or organisation that processes data on behalf of the controller. For example, a cloud provider that is paid by the pizza delivery service to store personal data on its behalf can be considered a processor. When the GDPR applies, there is always a data subject and always a data controller, but not necessarily a processor, because the data controller can also chose to perform all data processing activities on its own. If a processor is appointed, in principle, the data controller is responsible for the actions of the processor.
- Two parties that determine the purpose and means for processing personal data together will be considered *joint controllers,* and they will share the responsibilities imposed by the GDPR.
- If the processor contracts another party to process personal data on its behalf, that party will be considered a *sub-processor.* If the cloud provider hired by the pizza delivery service to store personal data contracts a number of data centres which provide storage space, these data centres are sub-processors. The processor should see to it that the sub-processor abides by the rules and obligations under the GDPR; ultimately, the controller is responsible for the conduct of both the processor and the sub-processor.
- If a controller or processor processes personal data about EU citizens, but does not have an establishment in the EU, it has to appoint a *representative*. The representative should be based on EU territory and serves as the main contact point

for that organisation within the EU, for example for data subjects that want to invoke their rights or for supervisory authorities in the course of their investigations.
- Many organisations processing personal data are obliged to appoint a *Data Protection Officer* (DPO). DPOs must ensure that the rules in the GDPR are respected by the organisations that have appointed them.
- Each Member State has to set up a *national supervisory authority*, usually called the Data Protection Authority. This is an independent but government-funded public organisation responsible for overseeing the applicability of and compliance with the GDPR by people and organisations processing personal data.
- Member States can also appoint more than one supervisory authority, for example a separate supervisory authority per region or province or a separate supervisory authority for specific sectors, such as the telecom sector. In that case, there should be one *main supervisory authority* which is the national supervisory authority that coordinates the actions of the various national data protection authorities and participates, on behalf of all national supervisory authorities of that Member State, in the European Data Protection Board. When a country only has one national supervisory authority, that authority is the main supervisory authority.
- All main supervisory authorities of each EU Member State participate in the *European Data Protection Board (EDPB)*. This Board can issue opinions and guidelines on the interpretation of the GDPR and can function as an arbitration mechanism when two or more national supervisory authorities have a conflict. Under the 1995 Data Protection Directive, the European Data Protection Board was called the *Article 29 Working Group*. This Working Group no longer exists.
- The *European Data Protection Supervisor* (EDPS) is the Data Protection Authority for the EU and advises on the processing of personal data by EU institutions. The GDPR does not apply when an EU institution itself processes personal data.

Data processing by EU institutions is covered by a separate Regulation which includes rules similar to the GDPR.

- When a company operates in more than one EU country and/or processes data about citizens of more than one EU country, each of the national supervisory authorities of those countries are considered a *supervisory authority concerned.* This means that they should be consulted by and have a right to object to the decisions taken by the lead supervisory authority.

- The *lead supervisory authority* is the supervisory authority concerned that takes the lead in overseeing the activities of an organisation in more than one EU country. The other supervisory authorities concerned follow the lead of this authority, but can submit objections to its decisions to the EDPB.

1. Introduction

The General Data Protection Regulation (GDPR) contains rules about when and under what conditions it is permitted to collect, store, analyse and use personal data. Virtually every person and every organisation processes personal data: an online advertising company, a governmental organisation that registers car ownership, a school teacher who gives grades to students or a private person posting a photo of her friends on Facebook.

The GDPR document has 88 pages, containing no fewer than 99 articles and 173 recitals that provide more background information on the articles. The GDPR contains rules on retention periods, the conditions for sharing personal data with others, rules for processing sensitive personal data and several obligations related to issues such as transparency, accountability and data security.

This book explains these rules in plain language. It discusses the situations in which the GDPR applies (Chapter 2), what the basic data protection principles of the EU are (Chapter 3), the duties of organisations that process personal data (Chapter 4), which rights citizens can invoke (Chapter 5) and how these rights and duties are enforced (Chapter 6).

This book is aimed primarily at private and public organisations that want to understand what rules they have to comply with; data protection officers who are looking for a quick guide to the data protection landscape; citizens who want to know which rights they can invoke, and how; and students who want to know what is in the GDPR, without having to plough through almost 100 pages of legal jargon.

This first chapter will provide important background information on the right to data protection in the EU and will introduce the main ideas behind it, it will explain what the new rules provided by the GDPR look like and why it is important to understand and respect them. If you are only interested to know what is actually in the GDPR, please go to Chapter 2 directly.

1.1 The who, what, where, when and why of the GDPR

Who? Europe is a continent of about 50 sovereign national states. It encompasses a complex web of supra-national organs and institutions, of which the difference between the European Union and the Council of Europe is the most important.

The European Union has adopted the Charter of Fundamental Rights, the General Data Protection Regulation and a large number of legal instruments in other fields, such as telecommunication law, agriculture, law enforcement and immigration. The European Court of Justice (ECJ) is the highest court of the European Union. Twenty-eight countries are members of the European Union (twenty-seven when the Brexit is finalised). The Council of Europe has adopted the European Convention on Human Rights (ECHR), which is overseen by the European Court of Human Rights (ECtHR). Forty-seven European countries are members of the Council of Europe. All EU Member States are also members of the Council of Europe.

Initially, the division of tasks between the Council of Europe and the European Union was clear: the Council of Europe focused on protecting human rights, while the EU, as the successor of the *European Coal and Steel Community*, was mainly concerned with economic and socio-economic issues. Gradually, however, the European Union has adopted rules and regulations on almost every aspect of society, including human rights. The Charter of Fundamental Rights can be seen as the constitution of the European Union; together with the ECHR, it is the highest human rights instrument in Europe. There is no official hierarchy between the two documents or the two courts, but informally, the ECHR and the judgments of the ECtHR take precedence over the Charter and the judgments of the ECJ.

The Charter of Fundamental Rights of the European Union contains rights such as freedom of religion, freedom of speech, the right to privacy and the right to data protection. The General Data Protection Regulation contains specific rules that detail how the fundamental right to data protection is guaranteed in the EU. The GDPR can be compared to a country's anti-discrimination law that lays down specific rules on how to interpret and apply the constitutional prohibition on discrimination. The constitutional doctrine has higher legal status than the law, just like the fundamental right to data protection in the Charter has priority over the GDPR.

EU laws such as the General Data Protection Regulation take precedence over national laws. If, for example, Italian law conflicted with the GDPR, the Italian law would be declared invalid and the GDPR would take precedence. Similarly, decisions by the ECtHR and the ECJ take precedence over decisions by national courts.

What? The new rules on data protection in the EU are set out in a Regulation: the General Data Protection Regulation. The old rules were set out in a Directive: the Data Protection Directive of 1995. The difference between a Regulation and a Directive has important practical effects.

A Directive is a document that is adopted by the EU but needs to be implemented by each Member State individually. Citizens can only rely directly on an EU Directive on an incidental basis and in principle have to refer to the national law that is based on that Directive. This means that although the general legal framework is set out by the EU, each country implements these rules slightly differently, according to its cultural and political standards.

In contrast to a Directive, a Regulation has direct effect. This means that citizens can directly rely on the Regulation. Member States do not need to implement the rules contained in the GDPR in their national laws. This harmonises the data protection rules across the European Union. Persons and organisations that process personal data have to respect the Regulation as such. The GDPR makes an exception to this rule on a small number of points, such as the processing of sensitive personal data, the processing of personal data of minors and the exceptions to the data protection framework that are allowed when processing personal data is necessary in a number of clearly defined matters of public interest. On these points, Member States are allowed to provide specific rules and there may be slight differences between countries.

Where? Of the 50 independent sovereign nations on the European continent, 47 are members of the Council of Europe. Only countries such as Belarus and Vatican City are not. This means that almost all European countries are bound by the European Convention on Human Rights, including such countries as Russia, Turkey and the United Kingdom, even after Brexit (Brexit means leaving the EU, not the Council of Europe). The European Union has far fewer Member States, namely 28. These are: Austria, Belgium, Bulgaria, the Czech Republic, Croatia, Cyprus, Denmark, Estonia, Finland, France, Germany, Greece, Hungary, Ireland, Italy, Latvia, Lithuania, Luxembourg, Malta, the Netherlands, Poland, Portugal, Romania, Slovakia, Slovenia, Spain, Sweden and the United Kingdom. Consequently, only 28 countries are directly bound by the General Data Protection Regulation and when Brexit is finalised, this number will drop to 27.

Nevertheless, the Regulation will have a broader effect for at least three reasons.

First, four countries – Iceland, Norway, Switzerland and Liechtenstein – are part of the European Free Trade Association. These countries participate in the European Single Market. Iceland, Norway and Liechtenstein have agreed that the GDPR should apply on their territory, while Switzerland has made a special arrangement (see section 3.5). There are also countries that would like to join the European Union and are therefore generally inclined to follow the rules of the EU. These are Albania, Montenegro, Serbia, North Macedonia, Bosnia-Herzegovina and Kosovo (there are also official negotiations with Turkey, but these have stagnated). Finally, there are overseas territories where the GDPR is directly applicable, such as former colonies of EU countries in South America, which are still part of their national territory.

Second, the GDPR applies not only to organisations based in the EU, but also to organisations based outside the EU that operate in the EU's market. For example, if a US company offers products through a website targeted at German-speaking customers (German being the main language of Austria, Germany and Switzerland) and processes personal data of its customers, it is directly bound by the GDPR, even though it might not have an establishment in the EU.

Third, the GDPR sets the highest data protection standard in the world. As these rules are equally applicable throughout the EU, personal data may be transferred from each EU country to every other EU country. However, in principle, it is not permitted to transfer personal data to countries outside the EU, as this would mean that the strict data protection rules would no longer apply.

There can be an exception to this prohibition if, on the one hand, after negotiations with the European Commission and after substantial changes to its national legislation, a non-EU country has adopted legislation that provides a level of data protection similar to that of the GDPR. The European Commission has so far recognised Andorra, Argentina, Canada (but only for commercial organisations), Faroe Islands, Guernsey, Israel, Isle of Man, Japan, Jersey, New Zealand, Switzerland and Uruguay as providing an adequate level of protection. A special arrangement has been made for the United States of America and there are ongoing adequacy talks with South Korea. Thus, a company operating on EU soil with an office in Poland and its headquarters in Israel may safely transfer personal data of EU citizens to its headquarters.

On the other hand, if a country does not have a data protection regime equivalent to that of the GDPR, a non-EU-based organisation may commit itself to upholding such a level of data protection. For example, if a Swedish and an Australian organisation want to share personal data, this is in principle prohibited, unless they sign a contract in which the Australian organisation commits itself to treating the personal data it receives under a data protection framework that is essentially equivalent to the framework provided by the GDPR.

Because most multinationals around the world want to do business in the European Union (the second-largest economy in the world) or with organisations within the EU, and because this almost by definition involves processing personal data, these organisations will need to commit themselves to the EU data protection regime, at least with respect to the processing of personal data about EU citizens and activities taking place on EU soil.

When? The Regulation was adopted in April 2016 and entered into force in May 2018. This gave organisations processing personal data two years to implement the data protection rules in their internal operations. The GDPR replaces the Data Protection Directive of 1995. In fairness, most of the rules contained in the GDPR were already present in the 1995 Directive. The reason for replacing the Directive was that it contained few possibilities for fines and sanctions for organisations that did not respect the data protection rules. This meant that not all organisations made it a priority to respect the data protection principles. Under the GDPR, this has changed and a sanction of up to 20 million euros or, for a company, up to 4% of its total worldwide annual turnover in the previous financial year, can be imposed for each violation, among other measures. That is why, from May 2018, most organisations needed to do two things: implement the rules that had been in place since 1995 and implement a number of additional rules provided by the GDPR.

Why? The reason for replacing the Directive with the Regulation was that there was a gap between law and practice. The Data Protection Directive already contained strict data protection rules, but these were only marginally respected by companies and governmental organisations. To remedy this problem, five changes to the data protection regime were made.

1. *Harmonisation of the rules*: there were substantial differences in the way EU countries had implemented the rules from the 1995 Data Protection Directive in their national legislation. One of the explicit goals of the 1995 EU data protection framework was removing obstacles to the transfer of personal data within the European Union, by laying down

one common level of data protection. However, because a Directive needs to be implemented by each Member State individually and because they have a margin of discretion when doing so, organisations still had to comply with different rules in, for example, Germany and the Netherlands, which hampered business operations. Consequently, companies often established their headquarters in the country with the most flexible interpretation of the data protection rules. This obstacle has been addressed by laying down the data protection framework in a Regulation instead of a Directive.

2. *Harmonisation of enforcement:* the second problem with the 1995 Directive was that enforcement of the data protection rules also took place at national level. Each EU country had to ensure compliance with the data protection framework on its own territory. Countries differed as to how actively they enforced the data protection rules; some had a well-equipped, well-resourced and well-functioning data protection authority, while others had understaffed data protection authorities with very limited powers of oversight and enforcement. Again, this allowed companies to place their headquarters in countries with a low level of enforcement, thereby practically circumventing the EU data protection rules. This problem is tackled in the GDPR by placing more powers of oversight and enforcement in the hands of EU bodies and by allowing national supervisory authorities to take action across the EU.

3. *Enforcement powers strengthened:* because there were few rules on sanctions and fines in the Data Protection Directive, not all boardrooms put data protection compliance at the top of their agenda. The GDPR tackles this problem by enabling supervisory authorities to impose high sanctions and penalties in case of a violation. The GDPR also gives the data protection authorities powers to act more stringently and effectively. The emphasis on enforcing the data protection framework has meant that the decision-making process regarding data protection within organisations has moved from the lower echelons to the boardroom.

4. *Distributed enforcement:* under the Data Protection Directive, the basic model for enforcement was that every EU Member State would install a governmental organisation tasked with overseeing the application of the data protection regime and sanctioning violations. Such a model was still viable in the 1990s, because the number of data-driven processes was limited. Like other sectors with a sector-specific supervisory authority, such as telecoms, finance and healthcare, it was still possible for a national data protection authority to oversee all or most data-driven processes on its territory. But this is no longer viable, because data processing is not limited to a specific sector or to a number of organisations. Rather, virtually every organisation and every person processes personal data. As it is impossible for one governmental agency to oversee all people and organisations on its territory, the GDPR moves the role of the governmental supervisory authority to the second tier. At the first level, organisations processing personal data are not only obliged to follow the data protection principles, they also have to create instruments of oversight and control within their organisation. Among others, they have to document all data processes within their organisation; do an impact assessment for riskier and larger-scale data operations in order to prevent and mitigate harm; and implement organisational and technical measures to ensure compliance with the GDPR. Many organisations also have to appoint an independent Data Protection Officer to ensure GDPR compliance. At the second level, the supervisory authorities have the role of assessing the extent to which organisations adequately oversee their own compliance with the GDPR. Not only can supervisory authorities sanction organisations that do not adequately protect personal data, they can also impose fines when organisations do not adequately monitor their own compliance with the data protection framework, whether or not any of the material rules and provisions have been violated.

5. *Less emphasis on individual control:* the 1995 Directive emphasised the rights of data subjects – the individuals whose personal data are processed. This created a problem, because most citizens do not keep tabs on all the data that are gathered about them via cookies, sensors, CCTV cameras and other devices. People who are unaware of the fact that their data are gathered will not invoke their legal rights. In addition, because data processing is so widespread in modern society, it is almost impossible for an individual to take control over her personal data. It is estimated that there are about 5,000 organisations that process personal data about an average citizen. It is impossible for any person to assess in every case whether an organisation has respected all relevant data protection rules and if it has not, to start legal proceedings to correct any violation. For example, if a citizen read the terms and conditions and privacy policies she has to agree with on the internet, this alone would take on average one to two months a year. That is why the GDPR not only strengthens the rights of data subjects and increases obligations of transparency for organisations processing personal data, it also gives supervisory authorities increased powers to take action against violations of the GDPR, independent of any complaint by an individual, and explicitly allows Member States to provide a framework for collective actions. In addition, the GDPR discourages organisations from relying on the consent of individuals for legitimating data processing activities.

1.2   When is the GDPR relevant?

Many people and organisations believe that the GDPR is not applicable to them, but this assumption is usually false. Almost every organisation and every person processes personal data. Here are some basic examples to give you an idea:

1. You have just started a pizza restaurant with a friend and keep track of customers' names, addresses and orders on an Excel sheet. In such a case, you are processing personal data about your customers and the GDPR applies to your company. A person's name, address and pizza preferences are all personal data.

2. You run a business with a staff of 10. You process personal details of your employees in connection with their salary, sick leave and pension. All these data are to be regarded as personal data. Importantly, some of these data, such as information about sick leave, are considered 'sensitive data', processing of which is only allowed under exceptional circumstances. If your business outsources the financial administration to an accountancy firm, the GDPR still applies to you; in fact, you are responsible for ensuring that the accountancy firm also adheres to the GDPR.

3. You have founded a local tennis club and act as chairman of the association. You keep a public website on which you post the match results of your members. The GDPR applies to you and provides rules on whether and under what conditions you are allowed to make public such information about your members.

4. You own a chocolate shop and introduce a loyalty card that allows regular customers to receive discounts on products and allows you to send personal advertisements based on their customer profile. The GDPR contains special rules on when and under what conditions you are allowed to make personal profiles of people.

5. As a general practitioner, you process medical data about your patients. The GDPR obviously allows doctors to process such medical data, but also stresses that additional security measures and safeguards need to be put in place, so as to ensure that the data do not fall into the wrong hands.

6. You own a personal website on which you post wildlife photos you make on your hiking trips and use cookies in order to allow personalised advertisements on your website. The

GDPR requires you to create a button on your website that allows visitors to immediately see that you are collecting personal data about them and to object to it.

7. You run a private archive on the history of your home town and have obtained a number of archives and documents from private institutions, companies and individuals. Even if you remove all the names of private individuals from these documents, they will still contain personal data. The sentence: 'Mister ████████ was the director of the local football club from 1979-1984 and was accused of murder in 1991' still contains personal data, as it is possible to identify this person even without knowing his name. The GDPR also applies to such indirect personal data.

8. You are based in Turkey and manage a foundation that supports small-scale art projects across Europe. When awarding scholarships to artists, you register their name, account number, address and other relevant information. The GDPR also applies to such registers and related documentation by organisations based outside the EU, at least where they refer to information about citizens from one of the EU Member States.

9. You run a US company and offer products or services to a European audience. You will have to abide by the EU data protection rules, even if you do not have an office in the EU.

10. You have an Instagram account and post pictures of yourself and your friends on a public page. The GDPR applies to you as you are processing personal data.

1.3 Why is it important to respect the GDPR?

There are several reasons why it is judicious to respect the GDPR, such as, but not limited to:

1. *Partner organisations:* it is increasingly important for organisations to know that their partner organisations respect the GDPR. When organisation A shares data with organisation B, which is not GDPR-compliant, the supervisory authority

can sanction both organisations and the data subject can hold them both liable. Consequently, most organisations do not want to do business with entities that do not adequately protect personal data.

2. *Customers:* privacy and data protection are hot topics and frequently dominate the news. Customers are becoming increasingly aware of their rights and are taking the protection of their data seriously. The protection of personal data is one aspect consumers take into account when deciding which organisation they want to do business with. If the organisation does not respect the GDPR, citizens may prefer a competitor or invoke their rights, which costs time and energy and often results in disappointed customers.

3. *Reputation:* adhering to the rules of the GDPR, or even granting customers more rights than is strictly necessary, can have a positive reputational effect. Just as a proactive environmental policy can be part of a corporate social responsibility strategy, promoting safe and responsible data processing can enhance an organisation's reputation. Conversely, violating data protection principles can result in considerable negative attention, with even a relatively small data leak leading to media headlines.

4. *Organisational structure:* many of the rules in the GDPR provide handy tools and standards for making data processing operations within an organisation smart and efficient. For example, ensuring safe and secure data storage is essential to block third-party access to critical information, personal data being an increasingly important asset of most organisations. Guaranteeing that data are correct and up to date, a duty provided for in the GDPR, ensures that analyses based on those data are of high quality. And the requirement to delete data when they are no longer necessary reduces storage costs and lowers the liability risk. In many respects, the data protection framework helps organisations to arrange their information flows optimally and lays down rules on good data governance.

5. *Sanctions and fines:* if all of this seems too soft, the Regulation gives a number of other good reasons to follow the rules. Citizens can go to court to hold organisations liable for violating the GDPR, and the national supervisory authority can impose sanctions and fines. There are situations in which fines of up to 10 and others in which fines of up to 20 million euros can be imposed. Some of the more important examples are discussed below:

Administrative fines may amount to: – **EUR 10 000 000 or,** – **for a company, up to 2% of total worldwide annual turnover in the previous financial year,** if this figure is higher, **in the following cases:**	Administrative fines may amount to: – **EUR 20 000 000 or,** – **for a company, up to 4% of total worldwide annual turnover in the previous financial year,** if this figure is higher, **in the following cases:**
The requirement to document all data processing operations is not met (this requirement will be explained in section 4.1)	One of the Fair Information Principles is violated (this requirement will be explained in section 3.2)
The obligation to implement policy choices in the technical infrastructure of an organisation is ignored (section 4.3)	Personal data are processed without a legitimate ground (section 3.3)
The obligation to do a data protection impact assessment is ignored (section 4.6)	Sensitive personal data are processed without a legitimate ground (section 3.4)
The obligation to appoint a data protection officer is ignored (section 4.7)	Personal data are transferred to a country outside the European Union without a legitimate ground (section 3.5)
The obligation to take technical and organisational security measures is ignored (sections 4.8 and 4.9)	The information principle is violated (sections 4.4 and 4.5)
The obligation to report a security breach is ignored (section 4.10)	One of the data subject's rights is violated (Chapter 5)

1.4   Ten misconceptions about the GDPR

There are a lot of fairy tales, misunderstandings and misguided ideas about the General Data Protection Regulation. 10 of the most prominent misconceptions are discussed below.

1. The GDPR aims to restrict data processing

Many people believe that the goal of the GDPR is to restrict or curtail processing operations that involve personal data. That is untrue for a number of reasons.

First, the EU data protection framework fundamentally aims to remove restrictions on data processing operations. As explained earlier, the European Union has been traditionally concerned with economic issues and the creation of a single market in the EU. For example, a Dutch farmer can sell tomatoes in Cyprus, because the rules for producing and selling tomatoes in the Netherlands and Cyprus are the same, as they are based on an EU-wide regime.

One of the problems that existed before the EU data protection framework was put in place was that each country had different data protection standards embedded in its national laws. This hampered the use and transfer of personal data, as a company could only transfer personal data from Germany to Italy if it ensured that it respected both the Italian and the German data protection regime. Companies operating in all EU countries had to comply with a different legal regime for each data processing operation, which created many barriers for internationally operating companies, not least because different national laws sometimes imposed conflicting requirements. Adopting a single EU-wide data protection framework eliminated restrictions on trade and data transfer, while ensuring a high level of data protection.

Second, the GDPR has two explicit aims. One is removing barriers to the free flow of personal data within the EU, and the other is protecting citizens' fundamental rights. Both of these aims should be considered when interpreting the rules in the GDPR. In essence, the goal of the GDPR is to facilitate the processing of personal data, as long as the rights and freedoms of data subjects are respected. When the Directive was still in place, the European Court of Justice made clear that national laws could not give the rights of citizens more protection than the Directive provided, if this was at the expense of the freedom of organisations to process personal data. The EU data protection framework lays down rules where both the rights of citizens and the freedom of organisations to process personal data are equally respected.

Third, the rules in the GDPR seldom prohibit specific data processing operations. In most cases, they lay down procedural safeguards and principles ensuring accurate and secure data processing operations. Most rules in the GDPR take the form of 'if you process personal data, be sure to ....' store the data safely, be transparent about it, inform the data subject when a data breach has occurred, etc. There are only a few rules in the GDPR that entail prohibitions, and even these prohibitions are relative. For example, the GDPR in principle prohibits the processing of sensitive personal data, such as information concerning a person's sexual orientation, race or medical history, but then goes on to specify 10 general exceptions, the gist of which is that if organisations have a legitimate reason to process these data, they can (section 3.4).

2. The GDPR framework is complicated

It is sometimes suggested that the EU data protection framework is complicated and too demanding for organisations that process personal data. The opposite is true.

The GDPR lays down very basic and intuitive rules that are in no way innovative or difficult to understand. If you process personal data about me, you have to inform me about it, unless you do not have my contact details. If you store personal data about me, please take reasonable security measures to ensure that hackers or third parties cannot easily access my data. If, based on these personal data, you take decisions that affect me, please ensure that the data are correct. And so on. Data protection principles are the equivalent of basic traffic rules, such as look to the left and right before you cross the street, reduce speed when visibility is poor and keep your distance when you are driving behind someone.

3. The GDPR codifies new rules and obligations

Another common misunderstanding is that the Regulation codifies new rules and obligations. After all, so the argument goes, the data protection rules date from 1995, the era when the number of databases was limited, Google and Facebook did not exist and mobile phones were the size of a large brick. That is why, so the argument continues, the old rules had to be updated and adapted to the modern, data-driven 21st century. When the GDPR came into force, many organisations implied that they would have to invest a lot of time, money and energy to ensure that their processes complied with the new data protection rules.

Again, this is untrue. All substantive rules have remained the same. All the data protection principles (Chapter 3) are the same, all substantive obligations for organisations already existed (Chapter 4) and there are only minor adaptions to the rights of citizens (Chapter 5). For example, although the term data portability is new, the 1995 Directive already gave the data subject the right to request, in an intelligible form, the data undergoing processing. The rights to access, information and copy already existed; the right to rectification and the right to file a complaint already existed. The right to be forgotten had already been adopted by the Court of Justice on the basis of the 1995 Directive. And the right in the GDPR not to be subjected to automated decision-making has remained virtually the same as the relevant provision from the 1995 Directive.

Consequently, the General Data Protection Regulation should not really be seen as an instrument that provides new and stronger data protection rules; its innovation vis-à-vis the Data Protection Directive lies in its mechanisms for enforcing the rules. The problem was not so much that the rules contained in the Directive were outdated, but that they were not respected. That is why the GDPR, on the one hand, obliges organisations to monitor their compliance with the data protection rules, to carefully scrutinise risky processing operations and to inform the supervisory authority when a data breach has occurred, and on the other hand gives supervisory authorities the power to impose substantial fines and sanctions on organisations that violate the data protection framework. The only provisions in the GDPR that are truly new are those that ensure that the rules and principles that have been in place since 1995 will be respected, but the material rules and principles themselves have hardly changed.

4. The GDPR is about informed consent

Many organisations stress that they follow the data protection framework because they have obtained data subjects' informed consent. This is a misguided interpretation of the GDPR for various reasons.

First, an organisation can be GDPR-compliant without ever asking for consent. Consent is only referred to in the GDPR with respect to three obligations: having a legitimate ground for processing personal data (section 3.3); having a legitimate ground for processing sensitive personal data (section 3.4); and having a legitimate ground for transferring personal data outside the EU (section 3.5). In each of these cases, consent is mentioned as only one of multiple grounds that can be relied on by organisations processing personal data. It is an option, but certainly not mandatory.

Second, the GDPR implements strict conditions for consent. Consent will only be deemed legitimate if the data subject knows which data are processed, why and by whom; if she actively gives consent; if consent is explicit and unambiguous; if consent is specific – I give consent for these specific personal data to be processed for this specific goal under these specific conditions – and if the data subject is truly free to refuse such consent. There are even stricter conditions for consent when it involves sensitive personal data or data about minors. By implementing such strict conditions, the GDPR explicitly discourages organisations from relying on consent as their ground for processing or transferring personal data.

Third, the GDPR further discourages organisations from relying on consent by implementing a number of additional standards. For example, the data subject can always withdraw her consent, so that an organisation no longer has a legitimate ground for processing personal data. Another is that the organisation bears the burden of proof with respect to the legitimacy of consent – it is not for the data subject to show that she was not adequately informed, was not free to withhold consent, etc., but for the organisation to prove that it adequately informed the data subject, that the data subject was free to withhold consent, etc. If an organisation has processed personal data relying on consent, but the conditions have not been met, a fine or sanction may be imposed. And if an organisation, despite all these discouragements, still relies on consent, the GDPR grants data subjects additional rights, such as the right to data portability, which is the right to ask the organisation to send all data provided by the data subject to a competitor and then delete the data.

Fourth, consent does not have any bearing on most principles and obligations in the GDPR. For example, organisations have to store data safely and securely. Even if a data subject consents to lower levels of data security, this principle still stands. This is similar to regulations on car safety. Even if a consumer wants to buy an unsafe car, regulations simply prohibit manufacturers from producing unsafe cars. Likewise, most rules contained in the GDPR do not require the consent of the data subject, nor can the consent of the data subject waive any of these obligations and requirements. Consent is simply irrelevant for most aspects of the GDPR.

5. If data are encrypted, the data protection framework does not apply

Another misunderstanding is that if personal data are encrypted, the data protection regime does not apply. The GDPR requires organisations to take measures to store personal data safely and securely. This does not by definition include encrypting the data, though such measures are encouraged. For example, when an organisation's database has been hacked and the personal data in it have fallen into the hands of a third party, the GDPR suggests that this is a clear data breach. However, if the organisation has implemented strong encryption measures, so that the hackers cannot actually use the data, the repercussions for the organisation will be minimal.

Encryption as such is not required, but can be one of the measures taken by organisations to lay down adequate technical safety and security measures (see in particular section 4.9). Taking adequate safety and security measures is only one of many requirements in the GDPR. These requirements apply cumulatively. As explained with respect to consent, the fact that an organisation has a legitimate ground for processing personal data (one of the requirements for legitimately processing personal data) does not mean that the other data protection principles, such as that data should be stored safely and securely and that organisations should document their data processing operations, do not apply. In the same way, the fact that organisations have adopted adequate technical safety and security measures does not have any bearing on the applicability of the GDPR or the various principles contained in it.

6. The GDPR is already outdated

Many people believe that the GDPR was already outdated the moment it was adopted, as it would not cope with our current data-driven environment. As explained, the basic data protection rules and requirements stem from the early 1990s, when the internet played only a minor role in daily life; Google, Facebook and Amazon did not exist; and processing personal data was still costly and tedious. In fact, most of these principles were adopted as far back as the 1970s. Consequently, so the argument goes, the GDPR is based on principles that are clearly unfit for the data-driven era. This argument is false on a number of accounts.

First, as explained, the GDPR sets out very basic duties of care and procedural safeguards, revolving around transparency, data security and having a purpose for processing personal data. These are minimum standards that, at least according to the EU, are so basic that they are not dependent on time or context. Just as it is always a good idea to manufacture safe and reliable cars, it is always a good idea to process personal data safely and ensure that they are correct and up to date.

Second, there are a number of rules that conflict with some of the practices of companies and governmental organisations, especially those that are experimenting with big data projects and large-scale data-driven innovations. For example, the GDPR requires organisations to specify a purpose before collecting personal data, while big data practices allow personal data to be gathered without a preconceived purpose. While the GDPR embeds the principles of data minimisation, big data revolves around gathering as much data as possible. And while the GDPR stresses that data cannot be used for purposes other than those for which they were gathered, big data thrives on the re-use of data for new and innovative products and applications.

Consequently, the GDPR certainly aims to prohibit some of the wilder Silicon Valley business models. This is not a matter of the data protection principles being out of date. Nor, as is sometimes suggested, were the Brussels bureaucrats wholly unaware of these business models and out of touch with reality when they adopted the GDPR. On the contrary, the EU legislator was well aware of these business practices and was determined to put an end to them. The choice that has been made is that, rather than adapting the data protection principles to these big data practices, these practices should adhere to the basic human rights and procedural safeguards that have been in place for decades.

The GDPR should therefore be seen in the light of the more general EU strategy to break US hegemony when it comes to data-driven innovation and the associated ethics (or the lack thereof). For years, the EU has promoted data-driven projects that followed its basic data protection rules, while US organisations in particular have done as they pleased. Now, the EU has called time on such practices and has laid down a broader policy to ensure that foreign organisations wanting to do business in the EU actually adhere to European norms and standards. The EU does this by imposing fines and sanctions through competition law and consumer law, by tackling tax avoidance, and now also through the GDPR that it has in its toolbox.

7. The GDPR will hamper economic progress

It is often suggested that the EU data protection framework is so strict that it will hamper economic progress. It is of course difficult to measure exactly what economic effect an EU law has, but there are four good reasons to believe that the GDPR will actually stimulate economic progress.

First, as explained previously, the Regulation does not aim to restrict processing operations, but rather to lay down a minimum framework with safeguards for fair data processing. Many of the data protection principles could actually reduce costs for organisations. Data protection requirements can help organisations to organise their data flows more efficiently, reduce storage costs, lower liability risks and ensure that decisions based on the data are more accurate and effective.

Second, as also explained, the explicit goal of the GDPR is not only to protect citizens whose personal data are being processed, but also to stimulate transnational data processing operations. One of the goals and the background of the EU data protection framework was an attempt to lower the barriers for cross-border data processing operations by laying down one common framework for the EU. By harmonising the rules to an even greater extent, the GDPR furthers this aim.

Third, the GDPR provides legal certainty to organisations processing personal data and legitimacy to data processing operations. If such organisations adhere to all conditions and requirements laid down in the GDPR, they know that they are acting legitimately. A legal framework can also generate societal support and public approval for data processing activities. Interestingly, now that more attention is being paid in the United

States to privacy violations by Facebook, Google and others, even Silicon Valley companies are calling for stricter US data protection laws. A comprehensive legal framework provides legitimacy, reduces public outcry and negative media attention, and thus facilitates a stable business model.

Fourth, as discussed above, the GDPR lays down new rules for enforcement and compliance. In particular, it places duties of compliance on data processing organisations themselves. Among other tasks, they have to document the data they are processing, as well as why, how and under what conditions they are processing the data; they have to appoint data protection officers, do a data protection impact assessment and report potential data breaches. This has led to the emergence of a whole new industry within the EU. Accountancy firms perform data protection audits, while specialised organisations offer certified officers and companies offer smart solutions and technical tools. This has made the GDPR compliance sector one of the fastest growing markets within the EU.

8. The GDPR places an unfair burden on SMEs

There is a belief in some quarters that the GDPR places an unfair burden on small and medium-sized enterprises (SMEs), such as companies with no staff or only a handful of employees. The argument goes that it is all very well for the big tech firms to comply strictly with the rules, but that it is far too much to ask of a small business that does not have the same level of knowledge, resources and manpower. This is untrue, because the GDPR has recognised this problem and explicitly relieves SMEs from a number of the burdens.

First, the General Data Protection Regulation stresses that account should be taken of the specific situation of micro, small and medium-sized enterprises, and all relevant regulatory institutions and supervisory authorities are encouraged to consider the specific needs of these smaller enterprises. For example, supervisory authorities are encouraged to engage in awareness-raising campaigns specifically targeted at these SMEs. In addition, the European Commission has the authority to adopt specific measures for micro, small and medium-sized enterprises.

Second, many duties and requirements under the GDPR depend on context. For example, a specific obligation applies and an organisation has to take certain measures 'taking into account the state of the art, the costs of implementation and the nature, scope, context and purposes of processing as well as the risk of varying likelihood and severity for the rights and freedoms of natural persons'. This is legal jargon for: the more data an organisation stores, the more sensitive those data are, and the longer the data are stored, etc., the stronger the data protection measures should be that the organisation adopts. This approach applies to the obligation to adopt a data protection policy (section 4.2), to take data protection measures by design and by default (section 4.3), and to take adequate technical and organisational security measures (sections 4.8 and 4.9). This means, for example, that a different level of organisational and technical security is expected from a small pizza delivery service than from a large tech company.

Third, SMEs are explicitly exempted from some of the obligations in the GDPR. Although organisations that process personal data are required to carefully document their processing operations (section 4.1), the GDPR stresses that this obligation does not apply to an enterprise or an organisation employing fewer than 250 people, unless it processes sensitive data or engages in risky data processing operations.

Fourth, there are a number of obligations linked to the risk involved in data processing operations, such as performing a risk assessment (section 4.6), appointing a data protection officer (section 4.7), and reporting data breaches (section 4.10). If a sole trader or small business only processes a small number of non-sensitive data, then that organisation is not obliged to carry out a risk assessment, appoint an officer or report a data breach.

Fifth, if the supervisory authority uncovers a violation of the GDPR, it will take into account the extent to which an organisation knew about the violation and could have prevented it. This means that typically, supervisory authorities will impose higher fines and penalties on large organisations than on small enterprises.

9. Data protection infringements will lead to high fines

Many people have heard about the fines and sanctions that can be imposed if a person or organisation violates the data protection framework. Certain media and self-proclaimed experts claim that if, for example, an organisation accidentally mails 20 customers CC instead of BCC, this will lead to a fine of millions. This is of course untrue.

First, imposing a fine is only one of the many tools in the national supervisory authority's toolbox. Typically, the supervisory authority will follow the steps of the escalation ladder, of which only the ultimate step is imposing fines and sanctions. First, the supervisory authority will use its investigatory powers, and then it may give advice to the organisation in question; if the organisation does not follow that advice, the authority may issue a warning; subsequently, it may temporarily stop an organisation from processing personal data until it has brought its operations into compliance with the GDPR. Only if an organisation fails to follow these instructions will the supervisory authority typically impose a fine. Obviously, the authority is authorised to impose a fine right away, but it will normally only do so in matters of negligence and with respect to large organisations that structurally ignore the data protection principles.

Second, when deciding on the amount of the administrative fine, the GDPR suggests that the supervisory authority should take into account, among other things, the nature, gravity and duration of the infringement; the intentional or negligent nature; the actions taken by the organisation to mitigate the damage suffered by data subjects; the degree of cooperation with the supervisory authority; the sensitivity of the data being processed; and whether or not the organisation itself notified the supervisory authority of the infringement.

Therefore, when there is a minor violation of the GDPR, the supervisory authority will generally not impose a fine or only a very small one. When there is a deliberate and structural violation of the GDPR by a large data-driven organisation that has ignored the advice and warnings of the supervisory authority, a high penalty may be imposed.

10. Data protection is privacy on steroids

The General Data Protection Regulation helps protect the fundamental right to data protection. Many people believe that the right to data protection is part of, or equal to, the right to privacy. That is incorrect.

Privacy is essentially about protecting a person's private life and traditionally covers a number of areas such as one's home, body and communications. The right to privacy is perhaps the oldest constitutional right there is, as it relates to the separation between the public and the private sphere. It stands on equal footing with other rights such as freedom of expression, freedom of religion and the non-discrimination principle. The right to privacy is contained in the UN's 1948 Universal Declaration of Human Rights and the Council of Europe's European Convention on Human Rights of 1950.

In the 1970s, a new right was added in some European countries and the United States: the right to data protection. The invention of this new right was connected with the emergence of new technologies, making it possible for the first time to create large electronic databases. One of the primary reasons for creating a new legal doctrine was that although these databases contained a large number of data about citizens, most information was not sensitive or private. Instead, such databases included very general and often public data, such as the number of cars owned; whether a person was a dog owner; when and where that person was born, etc. The right to privacy does not necessarily apply to the collection and storage of data that are neither private nor directly affect a person's private life.

The core difference between the right to privacy and the right to data protection lies in their scope. Privacy is wider, as it provides protection to a person's home, communication, body and reputation. But for its part, data protection provides protection to more data than the right to privacy does. While the right to privacy protects information when data processing has a substantial impact on a person's private life, the right to data protection applies to all data that relate to a person. Whether processing such information does or does not have an impact on a person is not relevant for determining whether the right to data protection applies. The only relevant question is whether or not the information relates to an identifiable person.

Data protection principles mainly specify general duties of care for data controllers. For example, the Fair Information Principles (FIPs) have been in place since the early 1970s and specify very basic principles, such as: do not collect more data than you need, store data no longer than necessary, store data securely, be honest and transparent about your processing operations, etc. Although the EU framework has been changed significantly since then, from the original legal instruments that were quite literally one-pagers to the GDPR of almost 100 articles, these rather basic principles are still the core of most data protection frameworks.

Although the right to data protection was initially still closely connected to the right to privacy, it has gradually become an increasingly independent doctrine, especially in the European Union. For example, while the 1995 Data Protection Directive still made explicit reference to the right to privacy, the General Data Protection Regulation does not mention it once. Commonly used concepts such as Privacy by Design, Privacy Officer and Privacy Impact Assessment have been renamed Data Protection by Design, Data Protection Officer and Data Protection Impact Assessment under the GDPR.

In addition, the European Union has accepted a separate fundamental right to data protection, disconnected from the right to privacy. While the European Convention on Human

Rights and the Universal Declaration of Human Rights only contain a right to privacy, the Charter of Fundamental Rights of the European Union, from 2000, contains both a right to privacy and a right to data protection. That is why, at least in the EU, the right to privacy and the right to data protection must be seen as two closely related but still separate rights, with the GDPR providing rules to protect the latter fundamental right.

Universal Declaration of Human Rights (United Nations, 1948)	European Convention on Human Rights (Council of Europe, 1950)	EU Charter of Fundamental Rights (European Union, 2000)
Article 12	Article 8 Right to respect for private and family life	Article 7 Respect for private and family life
No one shall be subjected to arbitrary interference with his privacy, family, home or correspondence, nor to attacks upon his honour and reputation. Everyone has the right to the protection of the law against such interference or attacks.	1. Everyone has the right to respect for his private and family life, his home and his correspondence. 2. There shall be no interference by a public authority with the exercise of this right except such as is in accordance with the law and is necessary in a democratic society in the interests of national security, public safety or the economic well-being of the country, for the prevention of disorder or crime, for the protection of health or morals, or for the protection of the rights and freedoms of others.	Everyone has the right to respect for his or her private and family life, home and communications.
		Article 8 Protection of personal data
		1. Everyone has the right to the protection of personal data concerning him or her.

Universal Declaration of Human Rights (United Nations, 1948)	European Convention on Human Rights (Council of Europe, 1950)	EU Charter of Fundamental Rights (European Union, 2000)
		2. Such data must be processed fairly for specified purposes and on the basis of the consent of the person concerned or some other legitimate basis laid down by law. Everyone has the right of access to data which has been collected concerning him or her, and the right to have it rectified. 3. Compliance with these rules shall be subject to control by an independent authority.

1.5 Conclusion

The General Data Protection Regulation applies to virtually all people and all organisations in the EU and most organisations that do business in the EU or have EU citizens as customers. The rules contained in the GDPR provide a basic framework for fair data processing, laying down rules, for example that data must be gathered for a reason; that data must be stored safely and securely; that persons about whom data are processed should be informed of that fact; and that if a data breach has occurred, the organisation should inform the supervisory authority.

The next chapter will explain in more detail when the GDPR applies. Chapter 3 discusses the backbone of the data protection framework and its main principles. Chapter 4 will give an overview of the specific obligations that organisations have to respect. Chapter 5 explains which rights data subjects can invoke and, finally, Chapter 6 discusses how the application of the data protection framework is monitored and how the rules are enforced.

2. When does the GDPR apply and to whom?

When dealing with data processing activities, the first question is of course whether the General Data Protection Regulation applies. To answer this question, five concrete steps should be taken. If all five criteria are met, the GDPR applies. If one or more of the criteria are not fulfilled, the GDPR does not apply. These five steps are:

(1) When personal data
(2) are processed,
(3) the EU has regulatory competence,
(4) and no exception applies,
(5) the GDPR applies to the data controller and, where relevant, the data processor

The five points are explained below. If you already know that the GDPR applies to your organisation or are only interested in the material provisions and substantive requirements in the GDPR, please go to Chapter 3 directly.

2.1 When personal data…

In general, the question is not so much whether a person or organisation processes personal data, the answer to which is almost always yes, but which of the data that are processed should be considered personal data for the purposes of the GDPR.

Personal data are information relating to a person:

– Personal data are data that refer to a person either *directly or indirectly*. Direct personal data, for example, are someone's name and home address. Indirect data are specific details that refer indirectly to a person, for example, 'the comedian that entered Italian politics with his Five Star Movement' is enough to identify Beppe Grillo, or the phrase 'the neighbour that has the red Ferrari' is typically enough to identify a specific person.

- Personal data, for the purposes of the GDPR, concern both *private and public data*. Therefore, the Regulation applies not only to information that has been kept private, but also to information that is available to anyone. The sentence 'that person over there, next to the lamppost, with the blue tie' is considered personal information, as it refers to a specific person.

- The GDPR applies to personal data that concern *sensitive information* (Mr White has prostate cancer), but personal data can also contain very *insensitive information*, such as a person's name or the fact that someone is wearing a blue tie. The sensitivity of the information is irrelevant when determining whether the GDPR applies, though it is relevant when determining the conditions that the GDPR lays down for processing the data (section 3.4).

- Personal data concern *identifying data* – information that allows you to identify someone directly or indirectly – but also *identifiable information*. The latter are data that do not identify anyone at present, but will do so in time. Suppose you have two databases with which you cannot identify anyone, but this would be possible if they were merged. In that case, the databases will be considered to contain personal data, even before they are merged.

- Importantly, it is not necessary to know the name of the person with the blue tie for information to be considered personal data. 'Identification' can be read as *'individualisation' or 'specification'*. If, for instance, a company tracks a person's computer though cookies and builds a profile on her, without knowing her name, address and private details, but having a very clear insight into her online activities, then this will be considered personal data. This also applies when the same computer is used by a small number of people, such as a family.

Organisations often wrongly claim that they do not process personal data because they use one of the following techniques:

- *Encryption of data*: as explained in section 1.4, many organisations stress that because they encrypt the data in their possession, the GDPR does not apply. This is incorrect. The data are still accessible to the person with the key. And because technology is making decryption ever easier, hackers can often decode or crack the encryption used. Encrypting personal data does not mean that the GDPR does not apply; however, using encryption is highly recommended because the GDPR requires that if personal data are stored, those holding the data should take adequate technical security measures (section 4.9).
- *Use of pseudonyms*: when using pseudonyms, the dataset does not contain the name of a person, but a personal code. Instead of categorising data in relation to 'Mrs Brown', she is given a code, such as '245X *! LK9' or 'Snow White'. Again, this is a highly recommendable technique to use in order to meet the security requirements set out by the Regulation, but it does not mean that the data are not considered personal data. After all, a pseudonym is a unique identifier and even without a name it is possible to identify or individualise someone.

Organisations can legitimately argue that they do not process personal data if one of the three following situations applies:
- *Information about non-natural persons*: the GDPR only applies when data refer to natural persons, meaning people of flesh and blood. When data refer to deceased individuals, such as 'Napoleon was a great leader'; when it refers to legal persons, such as 'Shell is destroying our environment'; or to inanimate objects and events, such as 'It will be 20 degrees Celsius tomorrow', the GDPR does not apply. However, many data referring to deceased individuals, legal persons, inanimate objects or events will also refer to natural persons indirectly. For example, the phrase 'Mrs White died of a hereditary form of breast cancer' also contains information about the daughter of Mrs White. When data are processed about a

small company with only three employees, information about that company, for example 'Bakery Brown & co. is in fact a criminal organisation', may be considered to relate directly to them.

- *Anonymisation of data*: if personal data are anonymised, the data protection regime does not apply. Anonymous means that the data can no longer be traced back to a person, as all so-called 'identifiers' have been removed. It is still important to stress that the reverse process, de-anonymisation, will often also be possible. Even with heavily anonymised medical data about patients, which have been used for scientific research, experiments have shown that data can be re-identified in a substantial number of cases. If re-identification or de-anonymisation is possible, the data cannot be considered anonymous. In general, so much direct and indirect, identifying and identifiable information has to be stripped to ensure a truly anonymous dataset that this will leave the database practically worthless. A common saying is therefore: 'Data can either be valuable or fully anonymous, but never both.'

- *The aggregation of data*: if data are categorised in groups with an n of, say, greater than 100, then in principle the GDPR does not apply. General statistical data such as 'Men are four times more likely to commit a crime than women'; 'In general, people with a big car have low self-esteem' or 'In city X, 70% of people are unemployed', as such do not fall within the scope of the GDPR. However, before the data are aggregated, they will often qualify as personal data, so that the General Data Protection Regulation applies at least to that part of data processing. In addition, when such broad categories are used to specifically address a person as part of a group, the GDPR will apply. For example, the information '70% of men with curly hair will buy product Y' will not be considered personal data, but when such information is used to categorise a specific person as a member of that group, in order to show him an advertisement of product Y, this will be the case. Finally, there is no precise border between non-aggregated and aggregated data. In general, the bigger the n, the more likely a dataset will be seen as falling outside the scope of the GDPR. But statistical information about a neighbourhood, for example, 'In neighbourhood Z, 80% of people will suffer from cancer due to the pollution from the nearby nuclear plant', can be considered personal data, if they can be linked to the people living in that area.

In conclusion, the scope of 'personal data' is wide. That is why more and more organisations simply treat all the data in their possession as 'personal data'. It often takes more time, energy and money to assess which data fall within the scope of the GDPR and which do not than simply to apply the data protection framework to all data.

2.2   ...are processed,...

The Regulation only applies when personal data are 'processed'. Processing is basically everything you can do with data. Not only collecting, storing, analysing and using the data, but also correcting, aggregating and even destroying, blocking and deleting data are considered 'processing'.

All data processed automatically or semi-automatically are subject to the GDPR, whether they are processed in a structured or unstructured manner. The GDPR distinguishes between automated data processing and analogue data processing. When data are processed with the help of a modern device, such as a computer, a smartphone, an IoT device, etc., the data will be considered to be processed for the purposes of the GDPR.

When data are processed manually, the GDPR applies when data are processed in a structured manner. Data are structured when they are stored according to a certain logic or when they are categorised or can be accessed using specific search queries. An archive will contain structured data and thus fall under the GDPR.

Only when data are processed in a non-automated and unstructured manner, will the GDPR not apply. A random scribble in a notebook can generally be considered to be unstructured and will thus fall outside the scope of the GDPR.

2.3   ...the EU has regulatory competence,...

The GDPR only applies to data processing activities over which the EU has competence. For example, when a company based in the United States processes information about US nationals, the GDPR will not apply. There are four situations in which the EU has regulatory competence:

1. The general rule is that the Regulation applies if personal data are processed by a person or organisation 'in the context of the activities of an establishment ... in the Union, regardless of whether the processing takes place in the Union or not'. If French citizen Ms Blanc publishes on the internet information about the sexual affairs of the French President, the EU has regulatory competence. If a French organisation processes personal data about a Greek citizen, the EU has regulatory competence. If an Australian fashion company with an establishment in Spain processes personal data of its Spanish customer, the GDPR applies. Having an 'establishment' implies the effective and real exercise of activities through stable arrangements. The legal form of such arrangements, whether through a branch or a subsidiary with a legal personality, is not the determining factor. Thus, when the person or organisation that processes personal data is based in the EU, the EU will generally have competence with respect to the activities undertaken in the EU.

2. Even when a person or organisation is not based in the EU, the EU will have regulatory competence when the person or organisation offers products or services to EU citizens and collects data about them. Whether a product or service is considered to be offered to EU citizens depends on the

context. If a US company with no establishment in the EU has an English-language website that is accessible to any citizen in the world, such as Amazon.com, the website will not necessarily be considered to be aimed at EU citizens. However, when the website is in German and has a German .de extension, the GDPR will typically apply, even when the organisation has no establishment in Germany. Similarly, when a non-EU-based organisation advertises its services explicitly to EU citizens, the GDPR will apply.

3. The EU will also have regulatory competence when a person or organisation is not based in the EU, but monitors the behaviour of EU citizens, insofar as their actions take place in the EU. If an EU citizen goes to China and she is observed there by a Chinese company or secret service, the Regulation does not apply. However, when a Chinese company observes the behaviour of EU citizens when they are in the EU, including their browsing behaviour, the Regulation does apply. So, if a Chinese company installs a cookie on the computer of an EU citizen and monitors her web activities and, for example, profiles her and offers her personal advertisements, the GDPR applies to that company.

4. Embassies and other international law organisations have a special status. A Portuguese embassy on foreign, non-EU soil that processes personal data will still fall under the EU data protection framework.

When the GDPR applies to a non-EU-based organisation (situations 2 and 3 above), that organisation must appoint a representative based in the EU to serve as the main contact point for data subjects and supervisory organisations. There is an exception to this requirement for private organisations if the personal data are processed only occasionally, on a small scale, and do not concern sensitive personal data or data processing operations that could pose risks to EU data subjects, and for government agencies (the presumption being that it will generally be easy to contact, say, the Tax Authority of a foreign country).

2.4   ...and no exception applies

If the three conditions of personal data, processing and EU regulatory competence have been met, the GDPR will apply, unless an exception applies. There are two types of exceptions to the EU data protection framework: categorical and partial exceptions. When a categorical exception applies, the GDPR is altogether irrelevant. Categorical exceptions can be further divided into two types. First, there are situations in which the EU does not have any regulatory competence. Second, there are situations in which the GDPR does not apply, but another EU data protection instrument will. In the case of partial exceptions, the GDPR does apply, but Member States may adopt limitations and exceptions with regard to particular rules and obligations in the GDPR.

The GDPR and no other EU data protection instrument applies:
1. When personal data are processed by a natural person (a person of flesh and blood, as opposed to a legal person), the GDPR applies when the goal of such processing is anything other than personal use. The GDPR does not apply when such data are processed solely for personal purposes. This exception is known as the 'household exemption'. For example, if you keep an address book on your computer or you have a physical photo album to which only you and your family members have access, the GDPR will not apply. Personal data posted on public websites do not fall under this exception, even in the case of a small blog, if anyone can access the data and consequently, the purposes for which the data are used cannot be limited or controlled. When personal data are published on a webpage with restricted access or a group profile that can be accessed by a small number of friends, the household exemption could potentially apply, though this would depend on the exclusive nature of the webpage or profile.
2. When personal data are processed for matters of national security, for example by secret services, the EU does not have competence and Member States have a prerogative in

this domain. Similarly, when personal data are processed by Member States while carrying out activities relating to foreign and security policy, neither the GDPR nor any other EU data protection instrument applies. However, this does not mean that national intelligence services are not regulated, only that no EU data protection regime applies. Each EU Member State has its own laws regulating its intelligence agencies, which contain rules on privacy and data protection.

The GDPR does not apply, but another EU data protection instrument does:

1. When EU institutions themselves process personal data. The EU does not have a fully-fledged governmental apparatus as national states do, but there are several institutions that process personal data, such as the European Central Bank, the European External Action Service, the European Economic and Social Committee, the European Committee of the Regions, the European Investment Bank, the European Ombudsman and, of course, the European Parliament, the European Council of Ministers, the European Commission and the European Court of Justice. When these institutions process personal data, a special data protection regulation applies, which more or less embodies the same principles as the GDPR. That regulation has installed a supervisory authority for EU institutions in the field of data protection, called the European Data Protection Supervisor (EDPS).

2. When a governmental organisation of one of the Member States processes personal data in the context of law enforcement, for example the police and judicial authorities, the GDPR does not apply, but the Law Enforcement Directive does. The Law Enforcement Directive was adopted at the same time as the GDPR, but being a Directive instead of a Regulation, it requires Member States to adopt national laws implementing the rules of the Directive in their legal systems, allowing for a margin of discretion. The Directive

recognises more or less the same data protection principles as the GDPR, but allows for more exceptions when these are deemed necessary in the fight against crime and public disorder.

The GDPR applies, but partial exceptions are allowed in the following instances:

1. Member States may adopt laws in which they limit the data subject's rights (discussed in Chapter 5) and the duty of organisations to inform the data subject of any data leak (discussed in section 4.10) for specific contexts on three conditions. On this point, Member States have a margin of discretion and the specific exceptions differ from country to country. The first condition is that the essence of these rights should remain intact. Second, the restrictions should be necessary and proportionate (section 3.1). Third, the contexts should relate to one of the following instances:
   a. national security;
   b. defence;
   c. public security;
   d. the prevention, investigation, detection or prosecution of criminal offences;
   e. other important objectives of general public interest, such as an important economic or financial interest, including monetary, budgetary and taxation matters, public health, and social security;
   f. the protection of judicial independence and judicial proceedings;
   g. the prevention, investigation, detection and prosecution of breaches of ethics for regulated professions;
   h. a monitoring, inspection or regulatory function;
   i. the protection of the rights and freedoms of citizens;
   j. the enforcement of civil law claims.
2. Member States may adopt laws in which they limit the data protection principles for certain contexts via a national law. Again, Member States have a margin of discretion and

the specific exceptions differ from country to country. The contexts that are exhaustively listed by the GDPR are:

a. *Freedom of expression and information:* for processing personal data in the course of a person's freedom of expression and information, including processing for journalistic purposes and for the purposes of academic, artistic or literary expression, Member States are allowed to make a special arrangement on almost all of the provisions in the GDPR (such as those described in chapters 3, 4 and 5), as long as these exceptions are necessary to reconcile the right to data protection with the freedom of expression and information, and as long as the Member State informs the European Commission of such special rules and regulations. This allows the European Commission to evaluate the necessity of such restrictions, and where necessary, to take action.

b. *Public access to official documents:* many EU countries have laws on open government and the re-use of governmental information. That is why the GDPR stresses that personal data contained in official documents held by governmental agencies or private organisations that perform public tasks (e.g. schools, medical institutions and railway services that are sometimes private organisations) may be disclosed when this is in accordance with the law.

c. *National identification number:* Member States may determine the specific conditions for processing a national identification number.

d. *Processing in the context of employment:* in the employment context, Member States are allowed to adopt special rules, for example to ensure that personal data can be processed for recruiting; organising work; assessing employee performance; promoting equality and diversity in the workplace; and ensuring health and safety at work, as long as those rules do not undermine a data subject's human dignity, legitimate interests and fundamental rights and as long as the Member State informs the Commission as to the laws it has adopted on this point.

e. *Processing for archiving or statistical purposes or scientific or historical research*: where personal data are processed for scientific or historical research purposes or statistical purposes, Member States may provide for derogations from the right to information (section 5.1); the right to access (section 5.2); the right to a copy (section 5.3); the right to rectification (section 5.5); the right to object (section 5.8); and the right to restrict (section 5.9). Where personal data are processed for archiving purposes in the public interest, Member States may provide for derogations from the same data subject's rights, with the addition of the right to data portability (section 5.4). These exceptions are only allowed if it would be very difficult or impossible to carry out the statistical, scientific or historical research when data subjects would invoke their rights and as long as adequate safeguards are taken to ensure that the interests of the data subjects are protected. For example, test subjects participating in a medical trial cannot have access to the data, because the test may depend on the subjects not knowing the reasons for the tests and their specific role in them.

f. *Obligations of secrecy*: Member States may adopt specific rules to set out the powers of the supervisory authorities in relation to controllers or processors obliged by law to observe professional secrecy, such as doctors. They can restrict the right of supervisory authorities to obtain access to all personal data and to all information such professionals need to perform their tasks or to obtain access to any premises, including any data processing equipment, with respect to the data that the professional has obtained under professional secrecy. This exception ensures that the data protection authority does not undermine the professional relationship, for example between doctor and patient. If Member States adopt such special limitations in their laws, they should inform the European Commission.

g. *Churches and religious associations*: if a Member State, prior to the GDPR, had special rules and regulations for the processing of personal data by churches and religious associations, these rules may continue to apply, as long as they are brought into line with the GDPR. In addition, the GDPR allows for a sector-specific data protection authority in this field, as long as it has the powers, competences and independence specified in the GDPR (section 6.3).

2.5 The GDPR applies to the data controller and, where relevant, the data processor

If the above criteria apply, i.e. personal data are processed, the EU has regulatory competence and no exception applies, then the GDPR is applicable. The question is who should uphold the principles of the GDPR. In principle, everyone involved should do so, though the GDPR makes an important distinction between two positions: that of the data controller and that of the data processor. The data controller controls the data process and is thus the main addressee of the data protection framework. The data processor processes the data on behalf of the data controller and should follow the data controller's instructions. There is always a data controller, but whether there is a data processor depends on whether the data controller has contracted another party to carry out part of the data processing operations on its behalf.

When more parties are involved in data processing, the GDPR sets out two criteria for identifying the processor and the controller. The party that determines (1) the goal of the data processing operations and (2) the way in which the data are processed is considered the data controller. If, for example, a law firm asks a cloud provider to store the data it processes on its clients, the cloud provider will be the data processor and the law firm the data controller. In principle, it is the law firm's responsibility to ensure that the cloud provider adheres to the GDPR, whether that processor is itself located in the EU or not.

After the GDPR was adopted, there were fierce discussions amongst organisations about who should be regarded as processor and who as controller. Some organisations were adamant that they should be the controller, because this would give them authority to decide what to do with the data and what not. Others actively tried to avoid being qualified a controller, because they wanted to avoid the burdens of the GDPR as much as possible. Such discussions are of some importance, but often much less so than people believe. There are a number of reasons for this:

– There is often no clear-cut difference between the organisation that determines the purpose and means of the processing operation and the organisation that blindly follows the instructions of the first. Often, both organisations have a say in the purpose and means of the data processing operation, or one organisation determines the goal and the other the means. In such cases, the GDPR specifies that both organisations will be regarded as controller – they are 'joint controllers', sharing the full responsibility for upholding the GDPR.

– Even when there is a clear-cut difference between the data controller and the data processor, the data processor is not relieved from upholding the principles of the GDPR. It mostly means that the controller outlines the policy and makes the choices and that the processor must respect those decisions. For example, the data minimisation principle and the principle of storage limitation, which imply that as few data as possible should be collected and that the data must be deleted once the goal has been achieved, only apply to the controller. However, this does not mean that the processor is not obliged to comply with these principles, but only that it must follow the instructions of the controller on how to respect those principles, for example on how long the data may be stored. Furthermore, if a processor knows or should have known that the controller makes choices that clearly contravene the GDPR, the processor should not cooperate.

- In addition, the GDPR specifies a number of independent obligations for data processors, such as:
  - Delete personal data when they are no longer necessary for performing the task you have been assigned by the controller. For example, if you have received a dataset from a controller in order to provide a statistical analysis, and after 1 year the contract is not renewed, you are not allowed to keep the personal data after that year for other purposes.
  - Document all data processing operations (section 4.1). For example, as the processor, you should document which data you process, why, who has access to the data, which technical and organisational security measures have been implemented, where the data are stored, etc.
  - Cooperate with any request from the data protection authority.
  - Notify the controller when a data leak has occurred (section 4.10).
  - In many cases, the data processor has to appoint a Data Protection Officer (section 4.7).
  - Assist the data controller in the performance of its task and duties, by following its instructions, by providing all relevant information to the controller and by respecting data subjects' rights when so instructed by the controller.
  - Adopt adequate organisational security measures (section 4.8), such as ensuring that employees within the processor's organisation only have access to those data that they really need for the specific tasks that have been assigned to them.
  - Adopt adequate technical security measures (section 4.9), such as encrypting and pseudonymising the data.
  - Comply with the relevant codes of conduct and certification mechanisms (sections 6.1 and 6.2).

- Do not involve another company or person in processing personal data without obtaining permission from the relevant data controller.
- Only use services from companies outside the EU, such as software, cloud computing or other digital services, if it is certain that these companies do not have access to the data and the data are not stored outside the EU, or if it is certain the GDPR is fully respected by that company.

– Besides the roles of data controller, data processor and joint controller, there are also other roles, such as that of sub-processor. The sub-processor is the organisation hired by the processor to execute part of the data processing operations. Take the case of a law firm hiring a cloud provider, in which the cloud provider contracts a data storage centre in Taiwan to store part of its data. The storage centre is then the sub-processor and the cloud provider is responsible for ensuring that the storage centre adheres to the principles of the GDPR.

– In essence, the GDPR is indifferent to who is a controller, a joint controller, a processor, a sub-processor, etc. For a citizen, it is important that the data protection rules are respected when personal data are processed; how precisely the respon-sibilities are distributed between the various parties is not. A data subject also wants to have a clear contact point and does not want to end up in a situation in which parties point to each other when she makes requests or invokes her rights. Not surprisingly, it is these two points that the GDPR underlines. Regardless of which parties work together in which capacity, they must always specify in a contract who has what role, who is responsible for which part of the data process, who will adopt what type of data protection measures and who can be held responsible for what part of the process. In addition, there must be one clear point of contact, not only for the data subject, but also for the supervisory authority.

– A supervisory authority may adopt instructions and impose fines and sanctions against both a data controller and a data processor.

- A data subject may lodge a complaint with the supervisory authority or start legal proceedings against both the data controller and the data processor.
- If a processor has failed to follow the controller's instructions or has violated any of its own obligations under the GDPR, the processor can be held fully liable for any damages that have occurred.

2.6   Conclusion

Five factors are relevant in assessing whether the General Data Protection Regulation applies to an organisation.

First, there should be personal data involved. Data are considered to be personal data when they refer to a person, whether the data are public or private, sensitive or insensitive, refer directly or indirectly to that person, etc. Given the broad scope of the term 'personal data', many organisations simply treat all data in their possession as 'personal data'.

Second, the personal data should be 'processed'. Processing is basically everything one can do with data, including correcting, destroying or deleting data. The GDPR does differentiate between the way in which the processing takes place. It does apply when processing takes place via automated means (e.g. through a modern device. i.e. computer, smartphone, IoT device, etc.); it also applies when data are processed via non-automated means, when the data are structured (e.g. a paper archive); it does not apply if data are processed via non-automated means, and they are not structured (e.g. a random scribble in a notebook).

Third, the EU should have regulatory competence. The GDPR applies to organisations that have an establishment in the EU and process personal data for the activities of these establishments. In addition, even when an organisation does not have an establishment in the EU, but offers goods and services directly to EU citizens or monitors their behaviour when they are in the EU, the GDPR will apply.

Fourth, there are several exceptions to the GDPR. When personal data are processed by natural persons (citizens) for purely private purposes or when they are processed by governmental organisations in relation to national security or common foreign policy, no EU data protection framework applies. When personal data are processed by EU organisations themselves or by national law enforcement authorities, such as the police, the GDPR does not apply, but another EU data protection framework does. When neither of these types of exceptions applies and the three previous conditions are met, the GDPR is applicable. In certain situations, Member States can adopt exemptions from parts of the GDPR in their national legislation. For example, the data subject's rights and the duty to inform data subjects of a data leak can be limited when this is necessary for reasons of national security, economic well-being or judicial independence. Also, Member States are allowed to lay down special regimes in their national laws for specific contexts, such as when personal data are processed by news media, contained in government documents that are made public, or used for scientific research.

Finally, if the GDPR applies, the question is to whom. Basically, all parties involved in data processing operations must respect the GDPR. If one party is clearly in control of the data processing operations – instructing (and typically paying) other parties to do part of the data processing on its behalf – that party is treated as the 'data controller'. This controller is responsible for ensuring that all other parties respect the GDPR's data protection principles and for laying down a policy specifying how the various data protection principles will be implemented.

Personal data	Processed	EU competence	Exception	Data controller
Personal data is any information	Personal data are processed when they are	Personal data are processed in the context of the activities of an establishment of a controller or a processor based in the EU; or	No EU data protection regime applies when personal data are processed by natural persons for personal reasons;	The person or organisation
about a living natural (non-legal) person	collected, recorded, organised, structured, stored, adapted, altered, retrieved, consulted, used, disclosed, transmitted, disseminated, made available, aligned, combined, restricted, erased or destroyed;	personal data are processed by an organisation not established in the EU, where the processing activities are related to the offering of goods or services to data subjects in the EU; or	No EU data protection regime applies when personal data are processed by governmental agencies in the context of national security or common foreign policy;	that alone or together
that can either directly or indirectly identify the person; or	through automated means, such as a computer, smartphone or any other digital device; or	personal data are processed by an organisation not established in the EU, where the processing activities are related to the monitoring of their behaviour insofar as their behaviour takes place within the EU; or	The GDPR does not apply, but another EU data protection framework does when law enforcement authorities process personal data;	determine(s) the goal and the means of processing personal data
can be used to identity her in the future; or	through non-automated means, when the data are structured, such as in an archive.	an embassy of an EU Member State on non-EU soil processes personal data.	The GDPR does not apply, but another EU data protection framework does when EU institutions process personal data;	shall be responsible for upholding the rights and obligations in the GDPR.
can be used to individualise her.			The GDPR applies, but Member States may make exceptions on specific points when in the public interest.	

3. What are the basic data protection principles?

This chapter briefly discusses the general principles at the heart of the GDPR. The duties (Chapter 4) and rights (Chapter 5) often follow from and elaborate on these general principles. This chapter will discuss these principles in five steps:

1. The core principle of the GDPR is legitimacy. The right to data protection is a fundamental right, contained in the Charter of Fundamental Rights of the EU. Fundamental rights may only be curtailed if this is necessary for a legitimate purpose and proportionate in relation to that aim (section 3.1).

2. The principle of legitimacy is further set out in the GDPR in 10 Fair Information Principles. These principles form the backbone of the Regulation and underline, among other things, that no more data may be collected than are necessary, that data must always be stored safely and securely, and that they must be deleted when the purpose for which they have been collected has been achieved (section 3.2).

3. Personal data may be processed on the basis of one of the six legitimate processing grounds listed in the GDPR, such as informed consent or a legal obligation to which the data controller is subject (section 3.3).

4. When sensitive data are concerned, such as information about a person's sexual preferences, race or medical condition, the GDPR specifies that in principle, processing these data is prohibited, except when one of 10 relatively broad exceptions provided by the GDPR applies (section 3.4).

5. Finally, personal data may in principle only be shared with persons or organisations within the EU. Sharing data with persons or organisations outside the EU is not allowed, except when these persons or organisations respect a level of data protection that is essentially equivalent to that offered by the GDPR (section 3.5).

3.1   Necessity, proportionality and subsidiarity

The right to data protection is a fundamental right. Fundamental rights are the highest rights that exist in the European Union and all other laws, rules and policies have to respect the fundamental rights framework. The fundamental rights are contained in the Charter of Fundamental Rights of the European Union. The Charter can be likened to the constitution of the EU, containing constitutional rights. The fact that these rights are the highest legal norms in the European Union does not mean that they cannot be restricted, but it does mean that such restrictions are only possible under strict conditions. The four basic requirements for legitimately curtailing any of the fundamental rights, such as freedom of expression, freedom of religion, the right to privacy and the right to data protection, are:

1. *Necessity:* restricting a fundamental right is legitimate only when it is necessary in order to achieve a legitimate goal. What is considered a legitimate goal in the data protection context will be explained in sections 3.2, 3.3 and 3.4. There is no general criterion to determine whether or not it is necessary to curtail a fundamental right; such evaluations depend on the context and the circumstances of the case. Suppose the police want to enter a house. If there is credible evidence that a notorious criminal is hiding in that premises or that a murder weapon may be found on the site, it will generally be deemed necessary for the police to enter that house. However, the police are not allowed to enter a house out of curiosity or precaution, to make people feel that they are being watched. It is this basic principle that is often ignored in the data protection context. For example, it is known that employees of organisations with large databases, such as the police or large medical institutions, often search for data about neighbours, family members, acquaintances or celebrities, out of interest. Such conduct is not legitimate: a 'nice to know' is not a 'need to know'.

2. *Proportionality:* even if it is necessary to process personal data for a legitimate purpose, data processing is allowed only when it is also proportionate to the legitimate purpose. If a very serious restriction of the fundamental rights of many people is required to achieve a marginal (yet legitimate) goal, it will not be deemed proportionate. In contrast, if a minor limitation is necessary to safeguard an important public interest, it will be deemed proportionate. Take the example of the police again. If the police have credible evidence that a terrorist is hiding in a specific house, they may of course enter. If they suspect that a terrorist may be present in one of the 10 houses in a street, as an urgent and exceptional matter they may enter all these houses. But they certainly cannot enter 1000 houses when they have received a tip that a terrorist is hiding somewhere in a small town. The same applies to processing personal data. If an organisation needs to collect large numbers of sensitive data to build a new web application that increases the user experience on its website, this would not be proportionate and thus not allowed. If a small number of non-sensitive data are required to provide an essential service, this will typically be deemed proportionate.

3. *Subsidiarity:* the third condition is the subsidiarity requirement. Subsidiarity is legal jargon for choosing the least infringing means to reach your goal. Suppose the police are pursuing a dangerous criminal. They are not allowed to shoot him right away. Only if the criminal does not respond to orders to stop and put his hands up are the police allowed to take action. Even then, the protocol is to first try to create barriers, for example by cutting off escape routes. If this proves fruitless, the police can be allowed to escalate by first shooting in the air. If the criminal still tries to flee, they may be allowed to shoot him in the legs and only as a last resort in vital parts of the body. The latter is still not permitted for an ordinary criminal, as such action would not pass the proportionality test, but could potentially be allowed in the case of an extremely violent criminal or dangerous terrorist.

The subsidiarity principle should also be respected when processing personal data. If an organisation can provide a service or product without collecting data, this is to be preferred over doing so by collecting personal data; collecting a small number of data is to be preferred over gathering large numbers of data; gathering insensitive data is to be preferred over gathering sensitive data; short-term data storage is to be preferred over long-term data storage; etc.

4. *Effectiveness:* finally, data processing must also be effective. This requirement follows from the necessity, proportionality and subsidiarity requirements. If the collection of data is ineffective or hardly effective in relation to achieving the intended goal, data processing will in general also not be deemed to pass the necessity, proportionality and subsidiarity tests. Nevertheless, it is particularly the principle of effectiveness that is often ignored in modern data processing operations. With the belief in big data, artificial intelligence and the Internet of Things, both private and public sector organisations have started many data-driven pilots and experiments, while research has shown that these experiments often show no or only minor results in terms of efficiency or effectiveness. Take, for example, predictive policing experiments, with which police agencies try to predict where and when criminal activities will take place by analysing statistical data about previous crimes and by extrapolating general patterns. Research has shown that such data-driven applications do not have any effect on crime rates or crime prevention. Likewise, in the private sector, data-driven projects are often terminated after one or two years because of their ineffectiveness. Under the EU fundamental rights framework, data-driven applications can in principle only be introduced if there is reason to believe that they would increase effectiveness or efficiency. If this is uncertain, the following steps should be taken:

a. Do a baseline measurement: what is the status quo before the introduction of the data-driven application?

For example, when introducing a data-driven app to increase customer satisfaction rates, first determine how satisfied the customers are before the introduction.

b. Establish goals: determine specifically what goal the data-driven application is intended to achieve. A specific goal can be improving the customer satisfaction rating from 4.9 to 7.9, or lowering crime rates by 10%.

c. Measure: assess after a year whether the goal has been achieved. If it has not, the project should be stopped, unless there are clear signs that adjustments will make the application effective. Even when there is a positive effect, for example when customer satisfaction rates have risen to 6.7, the question that should be asked is: is there a causal relationship between the introduction of the data-driven technology and the improved customer rating? Often, the introduction of a data-driven application is part of a broader strategy to increase customer satisfaction. It is not enough to point to the increase in customer satisfaction ratings to prove the effectiveness of the data-driven technology. For example, when predictive policing was deployed, some cities cried victory when crime rates dropped after a year or two; however, research showed that there was no causal relationship with predictive policing and that cities where the same technique was not applied had also seen their crime rates drop.

3.2   The Fair Information Principles

The General Data Protection Regulation regulates in further detail the fundamental right to data protection, similar to an anti-discrimination law at the national level implementing the constitutional right to be free from discrimination. Consequently, the four requirements discussed above also lie at the heart of the GDPR; the Regulation elaborates on them and provides more specific rules on what these requirements mean in the context of data protection.

The backbone of the GDPR is formed by the Fair Information Principles (FIPs). The early data protection instruments of the 1970s consisted mainly of these principles, which is why they were typically literally one-pagers. Gradually, data protection instruments have been extended and more specific rights and obligations were introduced in the 1995 Data Protection Directive and the General Data Protection Regulation. Nevertheless, the Fair Information Principles still form the basis of the GDPR.

The GDPR contains 10 Fair Information Principles. The data controller is charged with ensuring that these principles are respected.

1. *Lawful:* data processing must be lawful. This means six things.
   a. Data processing must be based on one of the six grounds enumerated in the GDPR (section 3.3).
   b. Sensitive personal data are not processed, unless one of the 10 exceptions enumerated in the GDPR applies (section 3.4).
   c. Transferring personal data outside the EU is not allowed, unless one of the exceptions enumerated in the GDPR applies (section 3.5).
   d. Data processing must naturally also comply with other applicable legislation, both at EU and national level, such as the national constitution, the Criminal Code and EU instruments in the field of competition law.
   e. An organisation may not process personal information it has obtained from third parties when it knows or should know that those parties obtained the data illegally.
   f. In principle, an organisation may not use personal data when it had no authority to obtain such information itself. For example, a police department may not circumvent rules and regulations that apply to it by hiring a private detective to perform certain data processing tasks.
2. *Fair:* data processing must be fair. To understand what is fair or unfair, one can think of unfair commercial practices that

mislead the consumer or unfair terms and conditions. A classic (hypothetical) example is the contract for the purchase of a watch which in the small print also includes an obligation for organ donation. A modern (alas non-hypothetical) example is providing in the terms and conditions of a flashlight app that the consumer also agrees to give more than 100 parties access to all the information, photos and videos stored on her smartphone. That is not fair and thus prohibited.

3. *Purpose specification:* data processing must serve a specific purpose.
   a. Firstly, this means that a goal must be established before processing personal data, not after data collection has started. Consequently, gathering data without a specific purpose and only evaluating the potential value of the data after they have been collected and analysed is not allowed.
   b. Secondly, that goal must be documented, for compliance and auditing purposes.
   c. Finally, the goal must be specific. A specific purpose is a pizza delivery service that processes personal data for the goal of 'delivering pizzas', for which it processes the name, address and orders of a customer. Although goals may be formulated in a slightly broader fashion than this example suggests, many organisations opt for too broad and general goals, such as 'customer contact', 'product improvement', 'innovation' or 'commercial activities'. These goals are too broad and will therefore be deemed unlawful under the GDPR.

4. *Purpose limitation:* data collected for a specific purpose may in principle only be processed for that purpose. Using those data for other, unrelated purposes is generally not allowed. For example, if the pizza delivery service decides to include sandwiches in its product range, it may use the data that were collected for 'delivering pizzas' for the purpose of 'delivering sandwiches'. However, it may not sell those data to an advertising company that wants to

use the dietary preferences of customers for selling food supplements. There is a rich and complex debate about which purposes can be seen as similar to and compatible with the original purpose. The GDPR provides five general criteria to determine whether re-use of personal data for different purposes is legitimate:

a. the link between the purposes for which the personal data have been collected and the purposes of the intended further processing;

b. the context in which the personal data have been collected, in particular the relationship between data subjects and the controller;

c. the nature and sensitivity of the personal data;

d. the possible consequences for data subjects of the intended further processing;

e. the existence of appropriate safeguards, such as encryption or pseudonymisation.

5. *Data minimisation:* the basic principle is that the smallest number of personal data should be gathered that are necessary for achieving the goal. The data minimisation principle is essentially a specification of the general necessity and subsidiarity principles discussed in the previous section. It simply means that a data controller may not collect more personal data than are strictly necessary to achieve the specific purpose. Therefore, if the goal is delivering a pizza, a person's name, address and order may be processed, but not her political affiliation, religious beliefs or country of birth.

6. *Accuracy:* personal data that are being processed should be and should remain correct and up to date. Importantly, this (and for that matter, the respect for all other FIPs) is the responsibility of the data controller and not of the data subject. The data subject can invoke her right or file a complaint if the data controller has not fulfilled its duties in this regard, but if the data controller fails to meet its obligation to ensure that data are and remain correct and

up to date, the supervisory authority may impose a sanction of up to 20 million euros, without any complaint from the data subject. This requirement entails that when collecting personal data about data subjects, the data controller must carefully reflect on the data it collects, how credible those data are and whether they are still accurate. For example, if it scrapes data from the internet, it should verify that the data obtained are reliable. When the data controller stores data for longer periods of time, it must do regular updates and checks to ensure that its dataset remains accurate and up to date. If, for example, an insurance company refused to sell someone an insurance policy based on faulty information about her risk behaviour or creditworthiness, this would be in violation of the GDPR. If the insurer charged an individual a higher price based on the postcode of the area she is living in, which has been categorised as a high-risk neighbourhood, but this address is no longer valid, this would be in violation of the GDPR.

7. *Storage limitation:* when the purpose for which the data have been gathered has been achieved, the data must in principle be deleted. If the purpose was 'delivering a pizza', the data should be deleted once the delivery has been made. A pizzeria can be allowed to retain the data after delivering the pizza in order to build a customer database. But if a person has not ordered anything for, say, a year, the data should be deleted. There are two exceptions. First, personal data may be retained after the purpose for which they have been gathered has been achieved when there is a legal obligation to do so, for example tax regulations requiring information storage for audits on cash flows, deliveries and income. Second, the data can be processed if used for statistical purposes, scientific research or historical research. Thus, if a university researcher did research comparing the food preferences of Italian and Austrian citizens, using the customer databases of 500 pizza delivery services in both countries, this would be allowed under the GDPR.

8. *Organisational security:* if the data are stored, for example in a database, register or file, the data controller has to implement organisational safety measures (section 4.8)
9. *Technical security:* if the data are stored, for example in a database, register or file, the data controller has to implement technical security measures (section 4.9).
10. *Transparency:* the processes of data processing must be transparent (sections 4.4 and 4.5).

As discussed, the first FIP requires personal data to be processed lawfully. The GDPR indicates what legitimacy means in three points. These will be discussed below.
(1) When is it lawful to process personal data? Discussed in section 3.3.
(2) When is it lawful to process sensitive personal data? Discussed in section 3.4.
(3) When is it lawful to transfer personal data to countries outside the EU? Discussed in section 3.5.

3.3   Legitimate processing of personal data

The General Data Protection Regulation lists six grounds on the basis of which personal data may be processed. If the processing of personal data cannot be based on one of these grounds, then that processing is unlawful and therefore in violation of the Regulation. But successfully invoking one of these grounds is enough to meet this specific requirement. The six grounds are:
1. The consent of the data subject;
2. A contractual relationship with the data subject for which it is necessary to process personal data;
3. The processing of personal data is necessary to protect a vital interest of the data subject;
4. A legal obligation under which it is necessary to process personal data;

5. A public interest for which it is necessary to process personal data;
6. The processing is necessary for the legitimate interests of the controller and those interests are more important than the interests of the data subject.

These grounds are briefly explained below; grounds 4 and 5 will be discussed in the same subsection.

3.3.1 Consent

Consent is one of six legal grounds a controller can base its processing operations on. Consent is seen as legitimate only if six conditions have all been met:

i. *Free:* first, consent must be freely given. If you as data subject are required to give your consent before obtaining a specific service, product or access to a website, this may mean that consent is not deemed to be freely given. This will be the case especially if you are required to obtain such a service or when there are no other viable alternatives to a service, product or website that can be regarded as essential. For example, many experts stress that when government websites ask users to consent to the use of cookies, such consent cannot be deemed to be freely given, as citizens cannot be reasonably expected not to use websites of government agencies and services. There is discussion about the extent to which there are viable alternatives to services such as the Google search engine and Facebook, and to what extent it is realistic to expect, for example, a teenager to do without Facebook or Instagram.

ii. *Specific:* in addition, consent must be 'specific'. This requirement follows in part from the purpose specification principle (section 3.2). As data subject, you must understand which data are gathered, for what specific purpose they are processed and why it is necessary to process these data in relation to that purpose. 'I agree to organisation X storing my contact details in order to send me a monthly newsletter', may be a specific form of consent. 'I agree to organisation X gathering all personal data it deems necessary for the purposes of product improvement, data analytics, consumer profiling and optimising internal processes' is not a specific form of consent and will thus not be deemed legitimate under the GDPR.

iii. *Informed:* for consent to be legitimate, it must also be 'informed'. As data subject, you must be told what data are processed, for which purposes and how they are used. The data controller must give you all relevant information in a concise and understandable manner. A 20-page statement in legal jargon is not appropriate; a half-page of information in simple language would suffice. If personal data about minors are processed, the data controller should attune its language and the format used.

iv. *Unambiguous:* consent must be unambiguous. First, this means that you should have undertaken an activity through which you consented. Inactivity, silence or an opt-out mechanism are not legal forms of consent. The minimum activity needed is for you as data subject to tick a box. Second, when the data processing serves multiple purposes, consent should be given for each of those purposes. Third, if you give consent in the context of a written declaration which also concerns other matters, the request for consent to process personal data should be presented in a manner which is clearly distinguishable from the other matters. For example, if a person buys a refrigerator online and the small print in the contract contains a paragraph stating that the data subject also consents to the supplier monitoring her food consumption, this would be in violation of the GDPR. At a very minimum, the consent for buying the refrigerator should be clearly separated in the contract from the consent to the processing of personal data.

v. *Burden of proof:* the data controller must be able to demonstrate the validity of the consent obtained. If you claim that data have been processed on the basis of invalid consent, you do not need to demonstrate such invalidity. It is for the data controller to prove that consent was obtained and that all conditions for legitimate consent were met.

vi. *Minors:* for minors aged 12 years or younger, consent in the online environment is only valid if it concerns parental consent. For data subjects aged 16 years or older, no parental consent is required; consent by a 16- or 17-year-old is valid, provided all other conditions have been met. For minors aged 13 to 15 years, the GDPR allows Member States to decide whether parental consent is required in the online environment. Some countries have opted to allow minors aged 13 and above to give consent without their parents' approval, while others have set the age limit at 16.

These very strict conditions make it hard for data controllers to obtain legitimate consent. The GDPR must be seen as explicitly discouraging consent as the preferred legal basis for processing personal data. Rather, consent should be the last ground organisations look to. They should first check whether any of the other legal grounds can be invoked and only then assess whether consent can be invoked. There are a number of additional incentives in the GDPR for not relying on consent as the legal basis for processing personal data. First, even if consent was legitimately given, the data subject can always withdraw her consent. That does not mean that in retrospect, data processing was illegitimate, but it does mean that if the data controller cannot rely on any of the other grounds, it must stop processing the data subject's personal data and, unless there are requirements to the contrary, must delete these personal data. Second, if the data controller relies on consent or contract as a legal ground, the GDPR grants the data subject additional rights, such as the right to data portability (section 5.4).

3.3.2 Contract

The second ground for processing personal data is related to and indirectly based on the data subject's consent, namely when processing is necessary for executing a contract to which the data subject is a party, or in order to take steps at the request of the data subject before entering into a contract. For example, if a person purchases a new, custom-made kitchen, she implicitly allows the company to measure, store and analyse details about her home. The necessity requirement means that only those data that are strictly necessary for the purpose of the specific contractual arrangement may be processed.

3.3.3 Vital interests of the data subject

Processing personal data may also be legitimate if it is necessary in order to protect the vital interests of the data subject. This reason plays virtually no significant role, because its scope is so limited. The core rationale behind this provision is that if the data subject could have given consent for processing her personal data, she would have. Two aspects are important to underline briefly.

1. What is a vital interest is not defined in the GDPR, but it is clear that such interests typically relate to health-related issues of the data subject. For example, if a person has a heart attack at home, it is legitimate for her neighbour to give her address to the emergency services. The GDPR also cites situations in which processing personal data may be both in the public interest and in the data subject's vital interest, such as when processing is necessary for humanitarian purposes, including monitoring epidemics and their spread or in humanitarian emergencies, in particular natural and man-made disasters.

2. This ground can only be invoked when none of the five other legal grounds can be. For example, if the data subject is capable of giving or withholding her consent, a data controller cannot rely on the vital interest ground. Thus, it can only be invoked when the data subject is, for example, unconscious or there is an emergency situation in which there is no time to ask for consent.

3.3.4   Legal basis and public interest

There are two grounds that are often discussed together. One is when processing personal data is necessary in order to comply with a legal obligation imposed on the controller. The other is when processing is necessary in order to perform a task carried out in the public interest or in the exercise of official authority vested in the controller. These two grounds typically apply to governmental and semi-public organisations. In general, when one of these two grounds applies to a situation, the other will, too. A specific legal obligation, for which processing personal data is necessary, is typically part of a law because it is deemed to be in the public interest. Conversely, the GDPR requires that processing personal data on the ground that it is necessary for performing a task that is in the public interest or in the exercise of official authority vested in the controller must always have a basis in either national or EU law. A data controller cannot decide on its own what is in the public interest; such a decision is left to the democratic legislator.

The GDPR does not specify which tasks are public tasks or which interests are public interests. Such decisions are left to national parliaments of the EU Member States and to the European Parliament. It is important to stress that European countries traditionally interpret public interests and tasks very widely, far more widely than, for example, the United States. Areas that are always considered public interests and public tasks (even when performed by private or privatised organisations) are education, security, healthcare, mobility, utility services, social welfare, housing and the judicial system. For example, although schools in some EU Member States are private organisations, they are strictly regulated as their activities are deemed to be in the public interest.

Because organisations may be subjective in deciding whether the data controller is carrying out activities based on a public interest, and because they may be rather quick to assert that this applies in their case, the GDPR gives data subjects the right to challenge the data controller's decision on this point (section 5.8).

3.3.5   Legitimate interest

Finally, the data controller can invoke its own interests as legal ground for processing personal data. This appears to be a very broad justification for processing personal data, but a number of important restrictions apply:

1. Public authorities cannot rely on this ground in the performance of their public tasks. In principle, they can only rely on grounds 3 (legal obligation) and 4 (public interest).
2. The interest must be 'legitimate', meaning, for example, that it must abide by the fairness principle and the other basic requirements of the GDPR.
3. The interests relied on by the data controller must be more important than those of the data subject.
4. The GDPR stresses that when one or more data subjects concerned is a minor, the data controller must be extra careful when invoking this legal ground for processing personal data.

Because determining whether the data controller has a legitimate interest which overrides the interests of the data subjects concerned is so subjective and because companies may be rather quick to assert that this applies to their case, the GDPR gives data subjects the right to challenge the data controller's decision on this point (section 5.8).

3.4   Legitimate processing of special categories of personal data

When sensitive personal data are processed, a special regime applies instead of the six grounds mentioned in section 3.3. When an organisation processes both ordinary personal data and sensitive personal data, it should have separate processing grounds for the two categories. Certainly not all organisations will process sensitive personal data. This section is relevant only to those that do and it will answer three questions:

1. What are special categories of personal data?
2. What is the ground rule with respect to processing this type of data?
3. What are the exceptions to that ground rule?

3.4.1 What are special categories of personal data?

Special categories of personal data, also called sensitive personal data, are data that reveal sensitive aspects of a person's life. The General Data Protection Regulation lists nine categories of special data. It contains no residual category such as, for example, Article 14 of the European Convention on Human Rights, prohibiting 'discrimination on any ground such as sex, race, colour, language, religion, political or other opinion, national or social origin, association with a national minority, property, birth or other status'. This means that if personal data do not fall in any of the nine following categories, they are not considered 'sensitive' for the purposes of the GDPR.

1. *Racial or ethnic origin*: information about a person's race or ethnic origin is considered sensitive personal data. The GDPR explicitly underlines that by giving this category of data a specially recognised status it in no way either explicitly or implicitly accepts or supports theories that determine the existence of separate human races, as was the case in Nazi Germany. Rather, the reverse is true, as the GDPR's aim is to avert, as much as possible, discriminatory practices based on race or ethnicity.

2. *Political opinions*: the political opinions of a person are also considered sensitive personal data. Most EU countries have controversial political parties such as far-right movements or communist parties. Membership of or affiliation to these organisations or movements may lead to negative repercussions, either from the government or, for example, from employers.

3. *Religious or philosophical beliefs:* information about the religious or philosophical (atheism) beliefs of a person also qualify as sensitive personal data. Religious and philosophical

beliefs are categorised as sensitive data because being a Jew, Muslim or atheist can, in some parts of the EU, lead to hatred, aggression and violence.

4. *Trade union membership:* membership of a trade union is also categorised as sensitive personal data. Some employers, for example, try to discourage their employees from joining a trade union or punish them for being members.

5. *Genetic data:* personal data relating to a person's inherited or acquired genetic characteristics can give unique information about that person's physiology or health. That is why the GDPR provides additional protection to genetic data as well.

6. *Biometric data:* personal data resulting from specific technical processing relating to the physical, physiological or behavioural characteristics of a natural person also qualify as sensitive data. Examples may be facial recognition, iris scans or fingerprinting, for which biometric data are typically used.

7. *Medical data:* personal data related to the physical or mental health of a natural person, including the provision of healthcare services, can reveal information about her medical condition. Such data are considered sensitive personal data. Health data may reveal serious diseases, such as cancer, schizophrenia or HIV/AIDS, but it can also involve a broken leg, migraine attacks or tinnitus. The bar is therefore quite low, though not so low that information about a person having the flu, a headache or a scratch will qualify as sensitive personal data.

8. *Sex life or sexual orientation:* a person's sexual behaviour, preferences or nature are among the most intimate aspects of her life, which is why they are categorised as sensitive data in the GDPR. Such data may include a person's sexual orientation, preferences for certain types of sexual activities, such as a leather fetish or love of sadomasochism, and actual sexual behaviour, such as making love in the bedroom, visiting prostitutes or going to a strip club.

9. *Criminal convictions and offences:* finally, information about a person's criminal activities or past is also categorised as

sensitive personal data under the GDPR. Data about past convictions for, for example, murder, theft or trespass, and information about current or future criminal acts qualify as sensitive personal data.

Two additional points should be made on this subject.

Firstly, sensitive data can also be inferred from non-sensitive personal data. The fact that two men are living at the same address is not in itself enough to determine whether they are gay, but combined with other non-sensitive data, such as their musical tastes or membership of and donations to a pro-*LGBTQ* movement, could be enough to derive accurate sensitive personal data.

Secondly, data about one person can say something about another person. This holds true for genetic data, but also applies to the other categories of sensitive data. When a mother is diagnosed with a hereditary genetic disease, this may also say something about her daughter. When two men live together and it is known that one of them is gay, it is quite likely that the other one is as well. If a person has a certain ethnic background, this says something about the ethnicity of her brother.

Consequently, the nine categories listed in the GDPR are quite broad and sensitive data may also be derived from indirect and non-sensitive data, so that these data, too, fall under the regime for sensitive personal data. Although not every minor aspect of a person's private life will be seen as revealing sensitive information, such as a scratch on a person's arm, the fact that a man is married to a woman or an 80-year-old stole a biscuit from her mother when she was 10, the threshold is quite low and revelatory data can include, for example, a broken leg, a leather fetish or any criminal conviction.

3.4.2 What is the ground rule with respect to processing this type of data?

The ground rule for data on criminal convictions and offences is that only governmental agencies, namely the law enforcement agencies, the public prosecutor and the judiciary, are allowed to process those data when they need to in order to perform their respective tasks. The rules governing the processing activities of these organisations are not included in the GDPR, but in a different EU data protection framework, called the Law Enforcement Directive (section 2.4).

For data that belong to any of the other eight categories of special personal data, the ground rule is that it is simply prohibited to process them.

3.4.3   What are the exceptions to that ground rule?

The GDPR provides exceptions to the prohibition on processing sensitive personal data. In general, there are exceptions when it is intuitively logical for sensitive personal data to be processed in a certain context. It is clear that a hospital may process health-related data, a political organisation may process information about the political affiliations of its members, and a dating app will have information about a person's sexual preferences.

The reverse is also true. If it is not intuitively logical and directly necessary for an organisation to process sensitive personal data, doing so is most likely prohibited. When hiring a new employee, a plumbing company cannot ask about a person's sexual orientation, a tennis club cannot process data about the political beliefs of its members and a local shop is not allowed to process the ethnicity of its customers.

There are 10 exceptions to the prohibition in the GDPR that a data controller can invoke when processing sensitive personal data. One of them must apply for processing sensitive data to be legitimate. These are:

1. *Employment and social security and social protection law:* Employers may need to process sensitive personal data in relation to an obligation under a law or a Collective Labour Agreement, for example registering sick leave or sensitive data in relation to pensions.
2. *Preventive or occupational medicine:* For an employer, it can be necessary to process medical data about employees. For

example, an airline may want to monitor the eye function of its pilots, and a construction company may want to pay extra attention to the joint function of its employees, in order to prevent permanent damage. Importantly, such information may only be processed by someone who is bound by professional secrecy, most likely the company doctor. This requirement prevents employers from abusing health information about their employees, for example by terminating the contract of employees with signs of joint wear.

3. *Church, political party or trade union:* In addition to the specific relationship between employer and employee, for which special rules apply, a church, political party or trade union may also process sensitive personal data, namely data regarding religious beliefs, political affiliations and membership of a trade union respectively. Such organisations must be non-profit organisations. Consequently, this exception cannot be invoked by companies that sell products or services to followers of a certain faith.

4. *Explicit consent:* Processing sensitive personal data is allowed when the data subject has consented. In addition to the various conditions for consent discussed in the previous section, when basing the legitimacy of processing sensitive data on consent, such consent must be *explicitly* given. This means that in order to be deemed legitimate for the purposes of the GDPR, consent must be even more specific, better informed and even more unambiguous than is normally the case.

5. *Manifestly made public by the data subject:* Processing sensitive personal data is allowed when a person has made that information public. For example, if a famous politician gave a major interview to a newspaper in which she came out as gay, she would manifestly be making such information public and implicitly accepting that others might also process that information. However, it should be stressed again that all other principles of the GDPR still apply, such as the necessity, proportionality and subsidiarity requirements. Importantly, manifestly making public sensitive information requires

a conscious and voluntary choice. It does not include, for example, making public one's religious conviction by wearing a headscarf or one's medical data by going into the public sphere wearing a bandage around one's arm.

6. *Vital interests of the data subject:* Just as processing personal data can be based on the protection of the vital interests of the data subject, this may also provide an exception to the prohibition on processing sensitive personal data. This exception can be invoked when the data subject is physically or mentally incapable of giving consent and is dependent on others to act in her best interests. Thus, this reason only applies when it is absolutely certain that if the data subject were capable of giving her consent, she would. For example, a relative providing the doctor with details of the data subject's medicine use after she has been involved in a car accident and is still unconscious.

7. *Substantial public interest:* Processing sensitive personal data can be necessary in the public interest. As with the notion of consent, the GDPR specifies an additional requirement for the public interest as grounds for processing sensitive personal data, compared to when it serves as legitimate ground for processing non-sensitive personal data, namely that a *'substantial public interest'* should be involved. Consequently, not every public interest can provide grounds for processing sensitive data.

8. *Public health:* Processing sensitive personal data is allowed when it is necessary in relation to a country's public health. This is an example of a substantial public interest that is listed separately in the GDPR. For example, a government may need to process sensitive personal information about an Ebola outbreak or other contagious diseases.

9. *Judicial proceedings and legal claims:* For the substantiation of a legal claim or a judicial decision, it may be necessary to process sensitive data. An example could be a claim for damages in connection with a car accident, of which medical data can form a central part. Or if two women are attacked

because they are walking hand-in-hand in a public park, such data may figure in the judgment of the court.

10. *Statistical analysis, scientific research and archiving:* Processing sensitive personal data is also allowed when necessary for archiving purposes in the public interest, scientific or historical research purposes or statistical purposes. These grounds can, for example, be invoked by university researchers, public archives and the official national statistical authority.

3.5 Legitimate transfer of personal data to parties in countries outside the EU

The General Data Protection Regulation also regulates the transfer of personal data from one of the EU countries to other parts of the world. On the one hand, the GDPR lays down a high standard for the protection of personal data throughout the EU. This means that although organisations have to respect all the principles contained in the GDPR, they can freely transfer personal data within the European Union, because the same level of data protection applies throughout the EU. On the other hand, the GDPR recognises that by imposing the highest standard of data protection in the world, transferring personal data to countries outside the EU would mean that a lower level of data protection would apply. That is why, in principle, the GDPR prohibits such transfers.

In addition to the 28 Member States of the European Union, three countries that are part of the European Economic Area (EEA) have committed themselves to EU data protection rules. These are:

- Iceland
- Liechtenstein
- Norway

Obviously, not all organisations that process personal data also transfer them to a country outside the EU, but many of them do. The concept of transfer should be interpreted broadly. It does not include all data published on the web, but it does include contracting services from technology companies that store or otherwise process the data in a country outside the EU. Therefore, the ground rule is that it is prohibited to make use of, for example, internet services or software from US or South Korean companies that use cloud computing to store the information in databases outside the EU.

However, as with the principle that it is forbidden to process sensitive personal data, the GDPR specifies a number of exceptions:

- First, an exception applies when a country has adopted laws that provide a level of data protection similar to that provided by the GDPR and when the European Commission has acknowledged this through what is called an adequacy decision.
- Second, the specific organisation to which data are transferred has signed a contract or legal document through which it commits itself to upholding a level of data protection similar to that provided by the GDPR.
- Third, when a small number of personal data are transferred on one specific occasion, an exception may be provided by grounds such as consent, a legal obligation or when such processing is necessary in the public interest.

Importantly, the rules contained in the GDPR on transferring personal data to non-EU countries also apply to onward transfers. For example, if it is legitimate to share personal data with an Israeli organisation, that Israeli organisation may only transfer the personal data it has received to another organisation based in a non-EU country, if one of the three exceptions to the prohibition on transferring personal data applies to that organisation.

3.5.1 Adequacy decision

In the first exception, a non-EU country may have adopted laws and policies which lay down a level of data protection essentially equivalent to that provided by the GDPR. In such a case, the non-EU country has to apply for an adequacy decision, through which the European Commission officially declares that a country has an adequate level of data protection. The European Commission only adopts such a decision after long negotiations and after the requesting country has made substantial revisions to its laws and policies. Such a process can easily take 10 years.

The European Commission has sole authority to decide whether a country has an adequate level of data protection. In doing so, it takes into account elements such as respect for the rule of law and human rights; whether the same principles as those embedded in the GDPR are respected; whether the country has adopted rules for the onward transfer of personal data to another third country; whether data subjects have effective and enforceable rights; and whether there is effective administrative and judicial redress for the data subjects whose personal data are being transferred. There should also be an independent supervisory authority in the country, with powers and competences similar to those of supervisory authorities within the EU.

At present, the European Commission considers only a small number of countries to have an adequate level of data protection. These are:

- Andorra
- Argentina
- Canada (for the commercial sector)
- Faroe Islands
- Guernsey
- Israel
- Isle of Man
- Japan
- Jersey
- New Zealand
- Switzerland
- Uruguay

There are also ongoing adequacy talks with South Korea. This means that with respect to these 12 countries, transfer of personal data is allowed, provided that all other principles in the GDPR are met. Transferring personal data from Italy (EU country) to Switzerland (adequacy decision) is like transferring personal data from France (EU country) to Germany (EU country). With respect to Canada, the adequacy decision is limited to the transfer of personal data to the commercial sector, for which there is a legal regime in place which has been deemed adequate by the European Commission. Transferring personal data to public sector organisations in Canada must in principle be deemed unlawful, unless other arrangements have been made.

There is a special arrangement for the US. The European Commission has not adopted an adequacy decision, but it has negotiated a self-certification mechanism. This allows organisations to self-certify; by applying for a certificate, an organisation can indicate that it adheres to an adequate level of data protection. This mechanism applies only to US organisations in the private sector, not those in the public sector.

Because there was virtually no assessment of whether companies that applied for the certificate indeed adhered to high data protection standards, many companies self-certified. A European citizen (Max Schrems) challenged that regime and the Court of Justice struck it down, finding it in violation of the fundamental right to data protection embedded in the Charter of Fundamental Rights of the European Union. Because of the relationship between the EU and the US and given the trade interests at stake, the European Commission fairly quickly negotiated another regime with the US, putting higher standards in place, while leaving the basic structure intact. This regime will be tested again by the European Court of Justice. The European Parliament has already suggested that this regime is inadequate and called on the European Commission to suspend the new legal structure. Until the Court of Justice has assessed the lawfulness of this regime, transferring personal data to US private sector organisations with a certificate must be considered lawful.

3.5.2   Legal arrangements

In the second exception, if there is no adequacy decision by the European Commission for a specific country, transfer to a specific organisation in that country may still be legitimate if it commits to a high level of data protection through a contract or another legal arrangement. Thus, although there is no adequacy decision for Mexico, an EU-based organisation may still be allowed to transfer personal data to a Mexican organisation if that organisation has committed itself to implementing and enforcing high data protection standards internally, which are similar to those provided by the GDPR. Such legal arrangement can generally be achieved in three ways:

1. Either the EU-based organisation and the non-EU-based organisation sign a legal contract or document that is based on, follows the template of, and includes the standard contractual clauses of a standard document, which is officially adopted and published by the European Commission, the European Data Protection Board or a national supervisory authority. In such a case, the specific details of the contract or legal document of the two or more organisations do not have to be submitted for review to, or scrutinised by, the European Commission, the European Data Protection Board or a national supervisory authority. Because they base their agreement on an approved standard document, this will be seen as providing adequate safeguards.

2. Or, if the EU-based organisation and the non-EU-based organisation do not want to base the transfer of personal data on a contract or legal document adopted by the European Commission, the European Data Protection Board or a national supervisory authority, they have to submit their legal arrangement for approval to the relevant supervisory authority. A common example is provided by the binding corporate rules, which an organisation can adopt for transferring personal data within a group of undertakings or group of enterprises engaged in a joint economic activity. The GDPR

specifies a number of principles and guidelines for such a joint economic activity.

3. Or, if the EU-based organisation and the non-EU-based organisation do not want to base the transfer of personal data on a contract or legal document adopted by the European Commission, the European Data Protection Board or a national supervisory authority and both organisations are in the public sector, such a transfer may be based on a document such as a law or by-law. This means that the document is officially published, can be enforced and can be challenged before a court of law. In such a case, the specific details of the contract or legal document of the two or more organisations do not have to be submitted for review to, or scrutinised by, the European Commission, the European Data Protection Board or a national supervisory authority, because the democratic legislator has sanctioned the agreement.

3.5.3 Occasional transfers

When either a country as a whole has put in place a level of data protection similar to that of the GDPR or a specific organisation legally undertakes to establish a level of data protection equivalent to that provided by the GDPR, transfer of personal data is allowed on a structural basis. The GDPR provides for a final exception to the ground rule that personal data may not be transferred to non-EU countries, namely when the transfer is for specific situations. The GDPR does not elaborate on what should be considered a 'specific situation', but in general, this concerns a one-time transfer of a small number of data, such as when a person orders shoes from an EU-based company and that company sends the person's shoe size and address to the manufacturer in India, so that the India-based company can manufacture the shoes and send them to the data subject's home. Such a transfer of personal data for occasional situations is allowed if it is based on one of the following grounds (which are similar to the grounds discussed in sections 3.3 and 3.4, which is why they will not be discussed in detail here):

1. It is based on the explicit consent of the data subject.
2. It is necessary for the execution of a contract with the data subject.
3. It is necessary for the conclusion or execution of a contract between the controller and another natural or legal person that is in the interests of the data subject.
4. It is necessary for important reasons of public interest. The GDPR gives as examples the international data transfer between competition authorities; between tax or customs administrations; between financial supervisory authorities; between services with competence for social security matters; or for public health, for example in the case of contact tracing for contagious diseases or in order to reduce and/or eliminate doping in sport.
5. When a court or an administrative authority of a third country requires a controller or processor to transfer or disclose personal data to an organisation outside the EU and either the EU or the Member State where the controller or processor is based has concluded an international agreement, such as a mutual legal assistance treaty, with that third country.
6. It is necessary in order to establish, exercise or defend legal claims.
7. It is necessary to protect the vital interests of the data subject. The GDPR gives as an example that if personal data of a data subject who is physically or legally incapable of giving consent is transferred to an international humanitarian organisation, with the aim of accomplishing a task that it has to perform under the Geneva Convention or of complying with international humanitarian law applicable in armed conflicts, this transfer could be considered necessary for an important reason of public interest or in the vital interest of the data subject.
8. The transfer is made from a register providing information to the public and open to consultation either by the public in general or by any person who can demonstrate a legitimate interest. This exception will not apply to the transfer of all

the personal data or entire categories of the personal data contained in the register.

9. It is necessary for the purposes of compelling legitimate interests pursued by the data controller which are not overridden by the interests or rights and freedoms of the data subject. There are three important conditions for this exception. First, the data controller cannot invoke any of the other eight exceptions. Second, the data controller must take additional measures to ensure that the rights and interests of data subjects are respected. Third, the controller must inform both the supervisory authority of the transfer and the data subjects concerned.

3.6 Conclusion

This chapter discussed the basic principles of data processing law. Data processing must respect the principles of necessity, proportionality, subsidiarity and effectiveness, must abide by the ten Fair Information Principles and one of the six grounds listed in the GDPR must apply. When an organisation intends to process sensitive personal data, the ground rule is that this is prohibited unless one of the ten exceptions specified in the GDPR applies. In addition, the ground rule is that personal data may not leave the territory of the EU, unless they are transferred to a country with a legal regime that provides a level of data protection similar to that of the GDPR, unless they are transferred to a specific organisation that commits itself through a legally binding document or approved legal arrangement to upholding a level of data protection similar to that of the GDPR, or unless the transfer is occasional and small-scale, and one of the nine grounds enumerated in the GDPR applies.

Fundamental Rights principles	Fair Information Principles	Legitimate ground for processing personal data	Legitimate ground for processing sensitive personal data	Legitimate ground for transferring personal data to non-EU territory
Personal data may be processed only if an organisation respects the principles of:	Personal data may be processed only if an organisation respects the principles of:	Processing personal data is deemed legitimate only when it is based on:	Processing sensitive personal data is not allowed unless it is based on:	Transferring personal data to non-EU territory is not allowed, unless it is based on:
Necessity; and	Lawfulness; and	Consent of the data subject; or	Employment and social security and social protection law; or	An adequacy decision; or
Proportionality; and	Fairness; and	Contract with the data subject; or	Preventive or occupational medicine; or	A legal arrangement between the EU-based organisation and the non-EU-based organisation; or
Subsidiarity; and	Purpose specification; and	Legal obligation on the data controller; or	Church, political party or trade union processing data about their members; or	Transfer is occasional and one of the following grounds applies: – Consent of the data subject; or
Effectiveness.	Purpose limitation; and	Public interest or task performed by the data controller; or	Explicit consent of the data subject; or	– Contract with data subject; or – Contract in the interest of data subject; or
	Data minimisation; and	Vital interest of the data subject; or	Manifestly made public by the data subject; or	– Public interest or task performed by the data controller; or
	Accuracy; and	Legitimate interest of the data controller overriding the interests of the data subject.	Vital interests of the data subject; or	– Order by foreign court or administrative body and international agreement in place; or
	Storage limitation; and		Substantial public interest or task performed by the data controller; or	– Establishment, exercise or defence of legal claims; or – Vital interests of the
	Organisational security; and		Public health interest or task performed by the data controller; or	data subject; or – Transfer is made from a register providing information to the public; or
	Technical security; and		Judicial proceedings and legal claims; or	– Compelling legitimate interests of the data controller overriding the interests of the
	Transparency.		Statistical analysis, scientific research and archiving.	data subject.

4. What are the duties of a data controller?

This chapter will discuss 10 specific obligations and requirements for individuals and organisations processing personal data. Before discussing these in detail, it is important to briefly highlight three points.

First, as explained in Chapter 1, a fundamental change the General Data Protection Regulation has brought about, compared with the regime in place under the Data Protection Directive of 1995, is that data controllers and processors are themselves primarily responsible for monitoring and ensuring GDPR-compliance. The supervisory authorities' role is to assess not only whether organisations are adhering to the substantive rules and obligations, but also to what extent organisations are adequately monitoring their own compliance with the GDPR. Not only can supervisory authorities sanction persons and organisations that do not adequately protect personal data, they can also impose fines when they do not properly monitor their own compliance with the data protection framework. This means that supervisory authorities are relieved in part of monitoring GDPR compliance and it ensures that basically all data processing operations are documented and evaluated by organisations themselves. The 10 duties can be roughly divided into two groups:

Substantive requirements	Compliance requirements
Informing the general public (section 4.4)	Documentation (section 4.1)
Informing the data subject (section 4.5)	Data Protection Policy (section 4.2)
Organisational security measures (section 4.8)	Data Protection by Design and Default (section 4.3)
Technical security measures (section 4.9)	Data Protection Impact Assessment (section 4.6)
Data breach notification (section 4.10)	Data Protection Officer (section 4.7)

Second, the GDPR is sometimes referred to as embracing a 'risk-based' approach, meaning that the application and interpretation of the rules and principles in the Regulation would depend on the risks at stake. This is untrue for most part of the GDPR; all rules and principles discussed in Chapter 3 and all rights discussed in Chapter 5 apply irrespective of the risk at stake. In addition, risk or harm is irrelevant when determining the applicability of the GDPR; as explained in Chapter 2, even writing in a blog 'Boris Johnson has beautiful eyes' would make the GDPR applicable. The only principles where risk, or rather, contextuality, is relevant is with the obligation discussed in this chapter. Even with respect to these obligations, this approach is neither new, as the same approach was prevalent in the 1995 Data Protection Directive, nor particularly remarkable, but rather evident and non-controversial.

For example, the GDPR specifies that the obligation to adopt a data protection policy and technical and organisational security measures is dependent on the context. This means that if an organisation processes high numbers of sensitive data, it should implement stronger security measures than when a local pizza delivery service processes the names, addresses and orders of its customers. Alternatively, when an employee of a pizza delivery service has accidentally sent an e-mail with the home address of a customer to a colleague who is not involved in delivering pizzas, the GDPR suggests that this is such a minor violation of the GDPR that the organisation will not be under a duty to inform either the national supervisory authority or the data subject concerned. A small organisation only processing non-sensitive data, to provide a final example, does not need to conduct a Data Protection Impact Assessment, appoint a Data Protection Officer or set up registers to document all data flows within its organisation. Consequently, the GDPR simply underlines that data controllers and processors are not under any obligation that is counter-intuitive. If it makes no sense for a small company processing only a handful of non-sensitive data to invest large sums of money in technical security, to lay down a detailed data protection policy, to conduct a full-fledged DPIA or appoint a DPO for two days a week, the GDPR does not require it to do so.

Obligation	Contextual element
Documentation (section 4.1)	The obligation shall not apply to an enterprise or an organisation employing fewer than 250 persons unless the processing it carries out is likely to result in a risk to the rights and freedoms of data subjects, the processing is not occasional, or the processing includes sensitive personal data.
Data Protection Policy (section 4.2)	Where proportionate in relation to the processing activities, the data controller shall adopt an appropriate data protection policy.
Data Protection by Design and Default (section 4.3)	Taking into account the state of the art, the cost of implementation and the nature, scope, context and purposes of processing as well as the risks of varying likelihood and severity for rights and freedoms of natural persons posed by the processing, the data controller shall implement data protection by design and by default measures.
Informing the general public (section 4.4)	–
Informing the data subject (section 4.5)	–
Data Protection Impact Assessment (section 4.6)	Where a type of processing in particular using new technologies, and taking into account the nature, scope, context and purposes of the processing, is likely to result in a high risk to the rights and freedoms of natural persons, the controller shall, prior to the processing, carry out an assessment of the impact of the envisaged processing operations on the protection of personal data.
Data Protection Officer (section 4.7)	The controller and the processor shall designate a data protection officer in any case where: (a) the processing is carried out by a public authority or body, except for courts acting in their judicial capacity; (b) the core activities of the controller or the processor consist of processing operations which, by virtue of their nature, their scope and/or their purposes, require regular and systematic monitoring of data subjects on a large scale; or (c) the core activities of the controller or the processor consist of processing on a large scale of sensitive data.
Technical and organisational security measures (section 4.8 and 4.9)	Taking into account the state of the art, the costs of implementation and the nature, scope, context and purposes of processing as well as the risk of varying likelihood and severity for the rights and freedoms of natural persons, the controller and the processor shall implement appropriate technical and organisational measures to ensure a level of security appropriate to the risk.
Data breach notification (section 4.10)	In the case of a personal data breach, the controller shall without undue delay notify the personal data breach to the supervisory authority, unless the personal data breach is unlikely to result in a risk to the rights and freedoms of natural persons. When the personal data breach is likely to result in a high risk to the rights and freedoms of natural persons, the controller shall communicate the personal data breach to the data subject without undue delay.

Third and finally, as explained in section 2.5, most principles in the GDPR are directed at the data controller. It is for the controller to uphold the principles discussed in Chapter 3 and the data controller is responsible for ensuring that the rights of data subjects discussed in Chapter 5 are respected. This does not mean that the data processor is not bound by those rights and duties, but only that it is for the data controller to decide whether, for example, to grant a request by a data subject to rectify her data (section 5.5) or how long data may be stored in light of the storage limitation principle (section 3.2), and for the data processor to follow those decisions. In addition, although some of the obligations discussed in this chapter apply and merely indirectly to data processors (such as that the data processor must assist the data controller in providing the data subject with all relevant information concerning the processing of her personal data), others apply directly to both the data controller and the data processor.

Applies to data controller	Applies to data controller and processor
Data Protection Policy (section 4.2)	Documentation (section 4.1)
Data Protection by Design and Default (section 4.3)	Data Protection Officer (section 4.7)
Informing the general public (section 4.4)	Organisational security measures (section 4.8)
Informing the data subject (section 4.5)	Technical security measures (section 4.9)
Data Protection Impact Assessment (section 4.6)	Data breach notification (where the data processor has to inform the data controller of any data breach) (section 4.10)

4.1   Documentation

If you want to make an organisation GDPR-compliant, the documentation requirement is a good place to start. Organisations have to document all internal data processing operations and record in a register which data are processed, why, for how long, with which parties data are shared, etc. When mapping data processes, organisations should assess and document whether they conform to the principles discussed in Chapter 3 of this book. If a data process does not conform to one of these principles, this compliance issue should be remedied or, if this is impossible, the data processing activities should be stopped. All new processes should also be documented and registered, and there must be regular checks to verify that all the documentation and information in the register are and remain up to date.

In its register, the data controller must at least record which data are processed; about whom; the purpose of the data processing operation; the legal ground for processing; the period, manner and conditions of data storage; with whom the data are shared; whether they are also shared with organisations outside the EU and if so, which safeguards are in place to ensure that a similar level of data protection is upheld as that provided by the GDPR. As far as possible, the data controller should also set out the planned time limits for deleting the different categories of data and provide a general description of the technical and organisational security measures adopted.

The processor has more limited duties regarding documentation, but also has to register which data it processes; with which organisations the data are shared; whether such data are shared with organisations outside the EU and if so, the safeguards applied; and, as far as possible, it must give a general description of the technical and organisational security measures adopted.

Most organisations also have more extensive registers in which they describe how the FIPs are respected for each data process and category of data. There are two additional points to note:

1. The register must be provided in written and electronic form.
2. The register should document the categories of data subjects and of the categories of personal data. Thus, a pizza delivery service does not have to document every datapoint separately, but can start by identifying, for example, three types of data flows (processing personal data of customers that order meals, of suppliers and of employees). Subsections should be made for clearly distinguishable data flows within those categories, for example in relation to employee data: the bank details processed to make salary payments, medical data processed for sick leave purposes, working hours recorded, etc. When there are clearly separate data flows serving different purposes or having clearly different roles within the organisation, each of these data flows must be registered and documented separately.

The documentation requirement has several goals. First, it forces organisations to scrutinise their data processing operations carefully and allows them to make these operations GDPR-compliant at an early stage. Second, it allows a quick response to data subject requests (discussed in Chapter 5), for example a request for information on the personal data being processed about them. Third, it allows data protection officers (discussed in section 4.7) to assess the various data processing operations within an organisation and analyse their GDPR compliance. Fourth, it allows the national supervisory authority to do audits and easily assess whether and on which point the GDPR has been violated (section 6.3).

Organisations with fewer than 250 employees are not required to document and register data processes. However, even these smaller organisations do have to meet this requirement if they:

1. Process sensitive personal data; or
2. Data processing is otherwise likely to result in risks for data subjects; or
3. Data processing is structural or permanent.

This means that organisations with fewer than 250 employees will also have to keep a register and document their data processing operations if they do more than just occasionally process personal data. What is occasional in this sense is not explained in the GDPR. A strict reading seems to suggest that very few organisations only occasionally process personal data, if only because they typically process personal data of their staff – even if they only employ one or two people. But given the meaning of and purpose behind this exception and given the fact that the GDPR explicitly lays down the threshold of 250 employees, it is safe to presume that this principle will not be interpreted so strict.

4.2 Data Protection Policy

The General Data Protection Regulation requires data controllers simply to adopt all technical and organisational measures necessary to ensure GDPR-compliance. These can include security measures (sections 4.8 and 4.9), but this obligation goes further than just securing the data. Organisations must take measures to ensure that all GDPR requirements are respected, such as the purpose specification, purpose limitation, data minimisation and storage limitation principles. One organisational measure to ensure compliance mentioned specially in the GDPR is adopting a Data Protection Policy (discussed in this section). A technical measure to ensure compliance mentioned specifically in the GDPR is implementing data protection choices by design and default in an organisation's technical infrastructure (next section).

The GDPR requires data controllers to adopt internal data protection policies and guidelines, which can include mandatory or prohibited activities by staff members, procedures and a division of responsibilities, such as which staff member is responsible for ensuring that personal data are actually deleted when the specified retention period has expired.

Data controllers that occasionally process non-sensitive personal data on a small scale do not have to formulate an internal policy. The more data that are processed, the more sensitive the data, the longer the data are stored, etc., the more extensive and the more comprehensive the internal policy must be.

The requirement of adopting a data protection policy is the only obligation that will not lead to an administrative fine from the supervisory authority if it is not carried out (section 6.3).

4.3   Data protection by design and by default

In addition to drawing up an internal policy, data controllers also have to ensure that the policy choices are embedded as firmly as possible in the technical infrastructure of the organisation. This can be done in two ways. In the first, the technical infrastructure can allow only a strict interpretation of the Fair Information

Principles (FIPs) and the other data protection principles – data protection by design. In the second, the technical infrastructure is based on a strict interpretation of the FIPs and the other data protection principles, but it is possible to deviate from them, for example at the data subject's request – data protection by default.

A non-exhaustive list of examples of privacy by design and by default measures:

1. *Retention period*: personal data are automatically deleted after one year (data protection by design), or personal data are automatically deleted after one year unless the purpose for which they have been gathered has not been met and the data protection officer agrees that the data can be stored for a longer period (data protection by default).

2. *Transfer*: it is made technically impossible to send personal data to countries outside the EU (data protection by design), or a red flag system is installed for when personal data are sent to countries outside the EU (data protection by default).

3. *Data quality*: personal data are automatically deleted if they have not been updated for more than a year (data protection by design), or the personal data are automatically deleted unless the data subject explicitly indicates that the data are correct and up to date (data protection by default).

4. *Reporting*: an automatic report is created when a staff member consults personal data and that report is forwarded automatically to the relevant data subject (data protection by design), or an automatic report is created unless the data subject indicates that she does not want to receive such a report (data protection by default).

The more data that are processed, the more sensitive the data, the longer the data are stored, etc., the more strongly the data processing principles must be implemented by design or by default within an organisation's technical infrastructure.

4.4   Informing the general public

Many organisations provide information about the type of data they process, how, why and which data protection measures have been implemented, through a privacy and data protection policy on a dedicated web page. As described in section 3.2, one of the Fair Information Principles is that the data controller must be transparent. The GDPR encourages transparency and openness about data processing operations in various ways, but there is no explicit obligation for an organisation to achieve transparency by publishing a privacy and data protection policy on its website.

The GDPR does require that data subjects be informed about the fact that their data are processed, and why and how (section 4.5). This requires a direct and individual form of communication. The GDPR does not prohibit an organisation from referring to a general privacy and data protection policy on its website, but it does require the data controller to take account of each individual data subject's specific situation when informing her about the data that are processed. Not only does the controller have to explain to each data subject exactly what data are collected in her specific case and why and how they are processed, but the form and content of the communication must also take into account the nature and background of the specific data subject with which the data controller communicates. For example, the controller must ensure that the information is clear and comprehensible to the data subject and must adapt the form and content of the communication if the data subject is a minor.

This means that the content of the information and the method of communication by the data controller may need to vary from one data subject to another. Consequently, although it is a good idea to have a general privacy and data protection policy on the website, a reference to it is often not enough to meet the obligation to inform the data subject individually (section 4.5).

The only situation in which the GDPR obliges the controller to provide information on a website or through another public channel, such as a newspaper, is if it is impossible to make contact with the data subject in order to inform her directly and individually (sections 4.5 and 4.10).

4.5   Informing the data subject

As data controller, you are obliged to inform the people whose personal data you are processing. The GDPR distinguishes two cases here – one in which the data are gathered from the data subject directly and one in which they are gathered through other means. In the first case, you obtain the data directly, either because the data subject provides them or because you directly observe the behaviour or activities of the data subject. In the second case, for example, you gain information about data subjects after data have been shared by another organisation.

For the first case, the following rules apply:

1. *Information:* the data controller has to provide the data subject with at least the following information:
    a. Its own identity and contact details and, where applicable, the contact details of its representative in the EU (section 2.3), and, again where applicable, the contact details of the data protection officer (section 4.7);
    b. The purposes of the processing for which the personal data are intended as well as the legal basis for the processing (sections 3.2 and 3.3 or 3.4), and further details on that legal basis;
    c. The period for which the personal data will be stored (section 3.2);
    d. Where applicable, the organisations with which the data are shared;
    e. Where applicable, the fact that the controller intends to transfer personal data outside the EU and the legal basis for that (section 3.5);

f. The various data subject rights (Chapter 5).
2. *Timing:*
   a. The data controller should inform the data subject before collecting the data.
   b. If the data controller intends to re-use already collected information for different purposes, it should inform the data subject before re-use.
3. *Exception:* when the data subject already has the information, the data controller is relieved from its duty to inform the data subject.

For the second case, when information has not been received from the data subject directly, the following rules apply:
1. *Information:* the information that the data controller should provide is basically the same as above, with the addition of having to tell the data subject how the data controller has obtained her personal data.
2. *Timing:* with respect to the time when the information should be provided, the GDPR makes clear that:
   a. The information should be provided at least within a month after having obtained the personal data;
   b. Or earlier than a month when the data are used to contact the data subject, in which case the information should be provided no later than the first contact;
   c. Or earlier than a month when the data are disclosed to a third party, in which case the data should be provided no later than the moment they are disclosed. If organisation B has obtained personal data from organisation A, and wants to send the data to organisation C, within one month after receiving the data, it should inform the data subject of this, just as organisation A, having obtained the data directly from the data subject, has a duty to inform the data subject of the fact that it will share her data with organisation B.
   d. If organisation B has obtained personal data from organisation A and it intends to re-use the personal

data for a purpose other than that for which they were obtained by organisation A, organisation B has to inform the data subject of this before re-using the data. If it does so within a month after having obtained the data, it should inform the data subject of that fact and provide her with all other relevant information. If it does so after a month, at a minimum, there should be two moments of contact – the first moment of contact is within a month, when the data controller should inform the data subject of all relevant information, and a second time, when the data subject should be informed of the fact that the data are intended to be re-used for new purposes.

3. *Exception:* the GDPR lists four exceptions to the duty to provide the data subject with the relevant information:

    a. When the data subject already has the information.

    b. When it is impossible for the data controller to reach the data subject or this would be too great a burden. In such a case, instead of informing data subjects directly and individually, the data controller should place information on a public website and, for example, publish a letter in a relevant newspaper, which is likely to reach a substantial number of the data subjects (section 4.4). This exception must be interpreted strictly. The GDPR refers by way of example to data processing for scientific and statistical purposes. For example, a university in Italy obtains a dataset from a Lithuanian archive, about the people who have visited the archive and which documents they consulted, with the names of the visitors but without their contact details. The Italian university wants to compare these data with statistical data about visits to Italian archives and it may be too much work to try and contact all the people in the Lithuanian database individually. Instead, the university can publish a letter in a Lithuanian national newspaper and refer to its public website for more information.

c. When the data controller is obliged by EU or national law to process the personal data (e.g. the Tax Authority receives personal data from the various governmental organisations providing social welfare) and the law contains appropriate measures to protect the interests of the data subjects.

d. When the personal data must remain confidential, due to an obligation of professional secrecy. For example, if a woman tells her doctor about her husband's domestic abuse, the doctor will obviously not be under an obligation to inform the husband of this fact, even though the information also concerns him.

4.6   Data Protection Impact Assessment

Doing an impact assessment, like appointing a data protection officer, is not mandatory for all organisations. National supervisory authorities may adopt a list of types of data processing operations for which an impact assessment is or is not mandatory. The GDPR gives four concrete situations in which a data controller is required to do a DPIA:

1. When sensitive personal data are processed on a large scale. This does not include the situation in which personal data from patients or clients are processed by an individual physician, other healthcare professionals or a lawyer. Healthcare institutions and law firms do have an obligation to do a DPIA when they process sensitive personal data on a large scale.

2. When large numbers of personal data about people's public behaviour are processed. The GDPR underlines that this is especially the case when optical electronic devices are used, such as X-ray machines or infrared scanners.

3. When personal data are processed for a systematic and extensive evaluation of personal aspects of data subjects through automated processing, such as profiling, and when decisions

are based on that profiling that have legal effects concerning the data subject. For example, a DPIA is required when banks or insurers develop risk profiles and categorise potential customers in these profiles in order to decide whether or not to provide a loan or insurance, and if so, under what conditions.

4. When another data processing operation is concerned which involves a high risk for data subjects.

Because the precise goal of the impact assessment is to assess whether there are any risks, most organisations carry out such an assessment for every data processing operation. To be on the safe side, many organisations have introduced the pre-DPIA, an assessment to analyse whether there are any risks involved and whether a fully-fledged DPIA is needed.

The GDPR also suggests that if the ground for processing personal data is a legal obligation or a public interest (section 3.3), then, when the law is being adopted which either contains the legal obligation to process personal data or the public interest on which the data processing is based, a general impact assessment can be done for data processing operations based on the legal obligation or public interest in general. When such a general assessment has been done during the legislative process, the data controller that bases its processing operations on that legal obligation or public interest does not need to do a DPIA.

Through a data protection impact assessment, an organisation assesses risks involved with a certain data processing activity and how to mitigate those risks. The GDPR stresses that if they cannot be mitigated, the data controller should consult the national supervisory authority on how to proceed. The authority can either advise the data controller to terminate the project or advise on the steps and measures that must be taken before the data controller can start the project.

Where possible, in the course of an impact assessment, the data protection officer, representatives of data subjects (for example, in the medical context, a patient representative) and other relevant experts should be consulted, such as an ICT specialist. The GDPR says little about the specific content of the DPIA, but the questions that are adressed will typically include:

1. Which categories of data will be processed?
2. What is the purpose of processing these data and to what extent are the data necessary and proportionate to that goal (section 3.1)?
3. What is the legal ground for processing these data (sections 3.3 and 3.4)?
4. Will the data be shared with third parties and why; if any of the third parties are located outside the EU, what legal ground underlies the transfer (section 3.5)?
5. How are the data processed and which data protection measures will be implemented to ensure compliance with the Fair Information Principles, such as taking security, data minimisation, pseudonymisation and storage limitation measures (sections 3.2, 4.2, 4.3, 4.8 and 4.9)?
6. How will respect for the rights of data subjects be guaranteed (Chapter 5)?
7. What risks does the intended data processing operation pose to the interests of data subjects?
8. Which specific measures are envisaged to address and mitigate these risks?
9. How effective are these specific measures likely to be in mitigating the risks identified?
10. Which decision is made on the go/no-go of the intended project and on what grounds?

4.7 Data Protection Officer

The GDPR requires all data controllers and data processors to appoint a data protection officer when:

1. The organisation is a governmental agency; or
2. The organisation profiles and observes citizens on a large scale, such as organisations that track citizens' online

behaviour through the use of cookies or companies that give credit scores or other ratings to data subjects; or

3. The organisation processes sensitive personal data as part of its core activities (section 3.4).

Organisations that in most cases do not have to appoint a data protection officer are sole traders and organisations that only process personal data on a limited scale, such as a plumbing company or pizza delivery service. However if a pizza delivery service uses its customers' personal data for profiling purposes and personalised advertisements, or if it processes sensitive data, such as their dietary preferences, or registers medical details, such as the fact that a customer has type 2 diabetes, the GDPR mandates that even that pizza delivery service must appoint a data protection officer.

As a result, many organisations are required to appoint a data protection officer, and in practice, most organisations of any size have appointed such a person, because this can help an organisation become GDPR-compliant and thus avoid reputation damage, claims by data subjects and potential sanctions from the supervisory authority. To support the trend towards every organisation having a data protection officer, the GDPR specifies that the officer can also be appointed part-time, for example one day a week, and that several organisations can share a data protection officer.

The data protection officer has various roles.

1. She serves as an adviser for the organisation and should be consulted when new data processing initiatives are on the table. A data protection officer is an expert in data protection law and can help assess risks, explain how the requirements in the GDPR relate to the planned processing initiative, and advise on best practices.

2. The officer is the first point of contact for data subjects who have questions or complaints regarding the way in which an organisation processes personal data. That is why the officer should be an independent employee of the organisation, which ensures that the questions and complaints are dealt

with neutrally and objectively. The officer's contact details should be made public, for example on the organisation's website.

3. The officer is the primary point of contact for the national supervisory authority. When the supervisory authority has questions about the organisation's data processing operations or wants to do audits, it will approach the data protection officer.

4. The data protection officer is also a mini-supervisory authority within an organisation. It can be seen as an extension of the national supervisory authority, assessing the GDPR compliance of an organisation, giving advice on how to remedy deficiencies and identifying risks to the rights and interests of data subjects within a particular organisation.

An officer must in any case meet the following cumulative conditions:

1. Competent: the officer must be competent and have expertise in the field of data protection law or related areas. An organisation cannot send its caretaker to a three-day GDPR training course and then appoint her as the data protection officer.

2. Independent: the officer is employed by, but still independent from, the data controller or processor. She can be compared to the company doctor, who is employed by the company, but is at the same time bound by professional standards and professional secrecy. Consequently, the data protection officer cannot have another role within the organisation that could lead to a conflict of interest. Although an organisation may, for example, appoint its head of legal affairs or its IT specialist as the data protection officer for two days a week, after having received the appropriate training, the GDPR prohibits someone from the management board, the head of the business and development department or the marketing specialist from becoming the organisation's data protection officer. In addition, the data

protection officer cannot be pressured by the board or staff of the organisation to take certain decisions or give positive advice. Nor can there be any repercussions for the officer if she acts or advises against the interests of the organisation. Finally, like a company doctor, the data protection officer is bound by professional secrecy, meaning that in principle, she cannot disclose the details of whistle-blowers within the organisation that have signalled GDPR violations, or the identity of data subjects that have filed a complaint against the organisation.

3. Resources and information: the officer must have adequate resources to carry out her tasks and duties. For example, the appointment of a data protection officer for 0.2 FTE within a large medical organisation would not be in line with the GDPR. The officer must also have access to all relevant databases, registers and files in which personal data are stored and she must be provided with all relevant information about the processing operation.

4. Involvement: the officer should be informed at an early stage of plans and decisions regarding the processing of personal data. She can advise on continuing or discontinuing plans and activities, on how to put adequate safeguards in place and on how a data subject's rights should be respected.

4.8   Organisational security measures

The GDPR specifies that both the data controller and the data processor must implement both organisational security measures (this section) and technical security measures (next section). Both obligations have the same aims: to ensure that data do not fall into the hands of either third parties (such as hackers) or employees that are not authorised to access the data, and to ensure that if they do, the risk of abuse is minimised. However, it is not enough for an organisation to take only organisational or only technological security measures. The extent of these measures depends on the sensitivity of the data processing operation. The more data are processed, the more sensitive the data are, the longer they are stored and the higher the risks to the interests of data subjects, the stronger the technical and organisational security measures must be.

There is no list of organisational security measures that you can go through to check whether your security regime is strong enough, but such measures could include:

1. *Authentication:* make sure staff can only access databases with a personal code. If an organisation works with sensitive data or high volumes of data, double authentication may be required, for example by having an employee scan her employee card and sending her an SMS on her mobile phone with a password, which she then has to enter.

2. *Access restrictions:* ensure that each personal code gives a specific employee access to only those data(bases) that the employee needs in order to perform her duties. The ground rule is that the bigger the database and the more sensitive the data, the fewer people should have access to it.

3. *Logging:* keep good records in order to know who has had access to data within the organisation. A logging mechanism could be introduced for employees who use their personal code to access data. This makes it possible to assess afterwards the reason and necessity for a specific access request. It is well known that some employees abuse their access rights, for example medical staff who are curious to find out the medical condition of a celebrity treated in their medical facility.

4. *Awareness training:* inform employees and customers about the methods of hackers and warn them about fake e-mails with requests for passwords or password resets.

5. *Clean desk:* insist that after working hours, all documents that are not safely locked away are put into the shredder.

6. *Physical security:* make sure that databases are physically locked and secured to avoid unlawful physical access by third parties.

4.9 Technical security measures

As with the organisational security measures, the GDPR does not provide a list of technical security measures that the data controller or processor has to implement; many organisations use the ISO standards on this point. The examples below can give you a rough idea of the type of technical security measures many organisations take:

1. *Automatic logout:* make sure that a computer to which an employee has logged in automatically logs out after a few minutes when it is not in use; this stops someone from using the credentials and access authorisation of another employee when she has left her desk.

2. *Security database:* prevent hackers from accessing databases by implementing strong technical security measures.

3. *Automatic blocking:* ensure that an alarm is automatically raised when multiple unsuccessful access attempts are made. The credentials of a person with three unsuccessful access attempts (failure to enter password or no response to the second authentication method) should be temporarily blocked; that employee should be notified and security personnel should assess the risk.

4. *Encryption:* make sure data is encrypted so that if a hacker or other third party gains unlawful access to a database, the data in it are encrypted, so that the unauthorised person cannot see and use them.

5. *Compartmentalisation:* place partitions between different databases within the organisation, each of which is at a different physical location, with data on different servers and secured through different technical measures, so that if hackers gain unauthorised access to a database, they only have access to a small number of data.

6. *Obstacles:* make sure that even if things do go wrong, you can block certain functionalities or throw up obstacles, so that if hackers or unauthorised personnel gain access to databases, it

is made difficult to copy, download or otherwise gain control over the data.

7. *Updates:* ensure that patches and software security updates are performed regularly.

4.10 Data breach notification

Finally, the General Data Protection Regulation contains an obligation to report a data breach. If the technical and organisational security measures have failed and data have fallen into the wrong hands, organisations may have the obligation to report the data security breach to the national supervisory authority and the data subjects involved. The GDPR identifies three situations:

1. *No risk:* data have fallen into the wrong hands, but this poses no risk or only a very minor risk to the interests of data subjects. For example, an employee of a pizza delivery service has accidentally sent an e-mail with the home address of a customer to a colleague who is not involved in delivering pizzas, or an employee of a local shop has lost a flash drive in a bus on her way home which contains the name of one of the suppliers of fruit sold in the shop. This is such a minor violation that the GDPR suggests the organisation will not be under a duty to inform either the national supervisory authority or the data subject concerned. Still, the GDPR requires the organisation to analyse how such an accident could have happened and whether it needs to update or revise its organisational or technical security measures (sections 4.8 and 4.9).

2. *Low risk:* if a data leak occurs that poses a risk to the rights and interests of the data subject, it must be reported to the national supervisory authority.
   a. Who? It is the responsibility of the data controller, but the data processor has the obligation to report a data breach within its organisation to the relevant data controller(s).

b. When? The data controller must inform the national supervisory authority immediately after it has learned of the data breach; if it takes longer than three days to inform the authority, the data controller must explain the reasons for this delay.

c. What? The supervisory authority must at least be informed of the nature of the personal data breach; the categories of data involved and the data subjects likely affected; the likely consequences of the data breach; and the measures taken or proposed to mitigate the possible adverse effects of the data breach and to prevent future data breaches.

d. Why? The national supervisory authority may instruct the organisation on appropriate subsequent actions to prevent future data breaches; advise the organisation to inform the data subjects; and possibly impose fines and other sanctions. The latter may be an incentive not to report a data breach to the national supervisory authority, but if such a breach comes to light, the failure to report it may in itself lead to a fine of 10 million euros, in addition to a potential fine for the data breach itself.

3. *High risk:* If a data breach poses high risks to the rights and interests of data subjects, they must be informed personally and directly. For example, when a data breach has occurred within a medical facility or bank, the organisation must inform its patients or customers that their data have fallen into the wrong hands. If the data breach could potentially have posed high risks to the rights and interests of the data subjects, but the organisation has taken either preventive measures, such as strong encryption making the data unintelligible to hackers or third parties, or has taken reactive measures, for example by destroying all data the moment unauthorised access occurred, the GDPR will consider that a high risk does not exist.

a. Who? This is the responsibility of the data controller, but the data processor has the obligation to report a data breach to the data controller.

b. When? The data controller must inform the data subject without undue delay.
c. What? The data subject should be informed of the fact that a data leak has occurred, which data have fallen into the wrong hands and what risks this entails.
d. Exception: the organisation may be exempted from its responsibility to inform data subjects when this is impossible or would lead to an undue burden. Suppose a university in Portugal has received a database from a Swedish smart city, with videos showing the faces and behaviour of residents, but without their contact details. In such a case, when those data are subsequently leaked, it may be too difficult to contact the thousands of data subjects. Instead of informing data subjects directly and individually, the data controller should place information on a public website and, for example, publish a letter in both a national and local newspaper that is likely to reach a substantial number of the data subjects (section 4.4).

Although the GDPR only requires a notification to the supervisory authority for a violation of the GDPR with respect to a data breach, most organisations inform the supervisory authority of all GDPR violations that have come to light, because if they do so on their own initiative, this will be taken into account when establishing the amount of the adqministrative fine or severity of the sanction imposed (sections 6.3 and 6.9).

4.11   Conclusion

This chapter has discussed 10 specific duties for organisations processing personal data. Most organisations have to document all data flows and databases within their organisation and describe, among other things, which data they process, why and how, how long the data are stored, for what purposes they are used, on which grounds processing takes place and which technical and organisational security measures have been implemented. Many organisations also have the duty to appoint a data processing officer to oversee GDPR compliance internally. When organisations engage in processing activities that could involve high risks for data subjects, they must identify these risks and specify how these risks will be mitigated. The national Data Protection Authority should be consulted if the risks cannot be mitigated. In addition, the controller has the duty to take appropriate technical and organisational security measures, develop an internal data protection policy and implement the organisation's policy in its technical infrastructure. Finally, organisations must be transparent, by being open about general aspects of the data processing operations performed, by specifically informing data subjects that their data are processed as well as how and why, and by informing the national supervisory authority or the relevant data subjects when a data breach has occurred.

Documentation	Data Protection Officer	Impact Assessment	Organisational and technical measures	Transparency
The controller and processor must document and register all data processes within its organisation, unless it is a small organisation processing non-sensitive data;	The GDPR requires all controllers and processors to appoint a data protection officer when: 1. The organisation is a governmental agency; or 2. The organisation profiles and observes citizens on a large scale; or 3. The organisation processes sensitive personal data as part of its core activities.	A controller needs to do a data protection impact assessment when: 1. Sensitive personal data are processed on a large scale; or 2. Large numbers of personal data about people's public behaviour are processed; or 3. Personal data are processed for a systematic and extensive evaluation of personal aspects of data subjects through automated processing, such as profiling; or 4. Data processing activities are likely to involve any other high risk.	The more data are processed, the more sensitive those data are, the longer the data are stored, etc., the more extensive the measures that data controllers and processors should adopt on the following points:	Data controllers should be open and transparent about the processing operations, for example through a data protection policy published on a public website; and
Each separate data flow, serving a separate purpose and having a specific role in the organisation should be documented separately;	The data protection officer has various roles. She is: 1. An adviser to the organisation; and 2. The first point of contact for data subjects who have questions or complaints; and 3. The primary point of contact for the national supervisory authority; and 4. A mini-supervisory authority within an organisation.	A DPIA will typically include: 1. Which categories of data will be processed? 2. What is the purpose of processing these data and to what extent are the data necessary and proportionate to that goal? 3. What legal ground is used to justify processing these data? 4. Will the data be shared with third parties and why, and if any of the third parties are located outside the EU, what legal ground applies to the transfer? 5. How are the data processed and which data protection measures will be implemented to ensure compliance with the Fair Information Principles? 6. How will respect for the rights of data subjects be guaranteed?	Develop policies in which it specifies how the various rules in the GDPR will be upheld within the organisation; and	The data controller should inform the data subject about the following information, unless this proves impossible: 1. Its own identity and contact details and, where applicable, the contact details of its representative in the EU, and, again where applicable, the contact details of the data protection officer; and 2. The purpose of the processing activities as well as the legal basis for the processing, and further details on the chosen legal basis; and 3. The period for which the personal data will be stored; and 4. Where applicable, the organisations with whom the data are shared; and

Documentation	Data Protection Officer	Impact Assessment	Organisational and technical measures	Transparency
		7. What risks to the interests of data subjects does the intended data processing operation entail? 8. Which specific measures are envisaged to address and mitigate these risks? 9. How effective are these specific measures likely to be in mitigating the risks identified? 10. Which decision is made on the go/no-go of the intended project and on what grounds?		5. Where applicable, the fact that the controller intends to transfer personal data to outside the EU and the legal basis for that; and 6. The various data subject rights. And;
The register should be kept in electronic form;	An officer should meet the following cumulative conditions: 1. She must be competent; and 2. Independent; and 3. Have access to all relevant resources and information; and 4. Be involved with the most important plans and decisions with respect to processing personal data.	The assessment can expose: 1. No or very limited risks, in which case the data controller can commence the intended data processing initiative. 2. Risks that can be mitigated, in which case the data controller can commence the intended data processing initiative after it has taken the appropriate measures to mitigate the risks. 3. Substantial risks that cannot be (fully) mitigated, in which case the data controller should ask the relevant data protection authority for advice and follow its instructions on either continuing the intended data processing initiative, discontinuing it or continuing it after the changes indicated by the authority have been implemented.	Implement policy choices in its technical infrastructure by design or by default; and	If a data leak has occurred, the data processor should inform the data controller; and

Documentation	Data Protection Officer	Impact Assessment	Organisational and technical measures	Transparency
What should be documented is: 1. Which data are processed; and 2. About whom; and 3. What is the purpose; and 4. What is the legal ground for processing; and 5. Which terms for storing data are used; and 6. With whom the data are shared; and 7. Whether they are also shared with organisations outside the EU, and if so, which safeguards are in place to ensure that a similar level of data protection is upheld; and 8. To the extent possible, the planned time limits for deleting the different categories of data; and 9. To the extent possible, provide a general description of the technical and organisational security measures adopted.			Adopt adequate organisational security measures; and	If a data leak has occurred, the data controller should: 1. Inform the national supervisory authority if there is a risk for data subjects; and 2. Inform the data subjects concerned if there is a high risk in relation to their rights and interests.
			Adopt adequate technical security measures.	

5. What are the rights of a data subject?

The General Data Protection Regulation assigns a number of rights to data subjects. These rights can be invoked vis-à-vis the data controller. When a data subject successfully invokes one of her rights, this often means that the organisation processing her data has violated the GDPR on another point, because most rights of data subjects correlate with the duties of data controllers. Consequently, in general, data subject rights do not add any substantive data protection requirement, but merely give tools to data subjects to mandate that data controllers indeed respect the obligations discussed in Chapter 3 and 4. It is important to stress that although data subjects can remedy GDPR violations by invoking their rights, data protection authorities can sanction those violations independent of any data subject right being invoked. Thus, although journalists, policy makers and laymen often emphasise the role of data subject rights, they in fact are peripheral to the EU data protection framework (for an overview, please check the table on the next page).

A number of general principles apply to all data subject rights and the handling of requests from data subjects.

1. *Free:* organisations cannot ask for money or other remuneration for fulfilling data subjects' requests. They have to respect all data subject rights free of charge; the only exception is the right to copy (section 5.3), for which data controllers can charge a reasonable fee based on administrative costs.
2. *Clear:* organisations have to communicate clearly with data subjects, using plain language in a common format. For example, a response to a question may not be written in technical or legal jargon, but must be understandable for an average person. When the data subject is a child, the organisation must take this into account when choosing the form, method and content of its communication.

Rights	Correlative obligations
Right to information (section 5.1)	The data subject can always rely on her right to information. However, if the data controller had adhered to its obligation to inform the data subject (section 4.5), this mostly would not have been necessary.
Right to access (section 5.2)	The GDPR encourages (but does not mandate) data controllers to make personal data permanently accessible for data subjects via digital means, so that they do not have to invoke their right to access.
Right to copy (section 5.3)	The GDPR encourages (but does not mandate) data controllers to make personal data permanently accessible for data subjects via digital means, so that they do not have to invoke their right to copy.
Right to data portability (section 5.4)	The right to data portability is perhaps the only right that does not directly correlate with an independent obligation by the data controller, though it can be seen simply as a combination of the right to copy and the right to erasure.
Right to rectification and completion (section 5.5)	If the data subject successfully invokes her right to rectification, this typically means that the data controller has violated one of the FIPs, namely to ensure that personal data are only processed when they are accurate and kept up to date (section 3.2).
Right to erasure (right to be forgotten) (section 5.6)	The data subject can only successfully exercise her right to erasure (right to be forgotten) if the data controller has processed her personal data unlawfully or without a legitimate ground, thus violating the basic principles of the GDPR (sections 3.2 and 3.3/3.4).
Right not to be subject to automated decision-making (section 5.7)	In principle, the data subject should not have to invoke her right not to be subject to automated decision-making, because this doctrine lays down an obligation for organisations not to subject natural persons to automated decision-making (similar to the right to non-discrimination at its core being a duty not to discriminate).
Right to object (section 5.8)	If the data subject's request to stop processing her personal data is granted by the organisation, this means, except where direct marketing is concerned, that the organisation has wrongfully relied on its legitimate interests overriding those of the data subject (sub-section 3.3.5) or on the public interest for which processing the data subject's data would be necessary (sub-section 3.3.4) as a legal ground for processing personal data.
Right to restrict (section 5.9)	The right to restrict applies only if one of the other data subject's rights is successfully invoked or when data processing is contrary to the GDPR.
Right to file a complaint (section 5.10)	If the data subject exercises her right to file a complaint and her claim is granted, this obviously means that the organisation processing her data did not act in line with the GDPR.

3. *Written:* communication takes place in writing unless the data subject explicitly requests oral communication. Written communication, in general, provides more legal certainty to both the data subject and the data controller.

4. *Digital:* as far as possible, organisations must ensure that data subjects can make requests digitally, for example via an online form or complaints procedure. Digital procedures help data subjects in making requests and invoking their rights; in addition, through an online form, the data subject can be required to provide specific information and details about the request, which makes handling such requests easier and more efficient.

5. *Time path decision:* the data controller must inform the data subject of the decision taken as soon as possible and in any case within a month after a request has been made.

6. *Extension:* depending on the number of requests and their complexity, the time path for responding to requests from data subjects may be extended by two months if necessary. The data subject must be informed within a month after she has made her request that the time path for responding to the request will be extended.

7. *Identity verification:* the controller is allowed to request additional information to verify the data subject's identity; if it cannot successfully identify a data subject, it may choose not to grant the data subject's request. This principle is laid down in the GDPR to prevent malicious third parties from obtaining information about a data subject, such as criminals calling a bank to get the login codes of a wealthy person, or a jealous ex looking for information to blackmail a former lover. This exception is important, because the GDPR makes it clear that if the purposes for which a controller is processing personal data do not or no longer require the identification of a data subject by the controller, the controller will not be obliged to maintain, acquire or process additional information in order to identify the data subject for the sole purpose of complying with the data subject's requests. In

such instance, it is for the data subject to produce sufficient information for the data controller to verify her identity.

8. *Exception:* the fact that a data subject has a right and makes a request does not mean that the data controller must follow that request. Some rights have specific exceptions, which will be discussed individually in the sections below. In addition, the GDPR contains a general exception, applicable to all data subjects' rights. If a data subject's requests are clearly unfounded or excessive, in particular because of their repetitive character, the data controller may either:
   a. Request reasonable compensation for the administrative costs associated with dealing with the requests.
   b. Refuse to comply with the request.

   It is up to the controller to substantiate the unfounded or excessive nature of the request. This exception prevents data subjects from abusing their rights, for example by submitting hundreds of requests in the hopes that the data controller will not respond (or not on time), so that she can go to court and claim financial compensation for the GDPR violation.

9. *Negative decision:* in case of a negative decision, the data subject should be informed of the reasons for the decision and the right of the data subject to submit a complaint against the data controller to the national supervisory authority or a court of law (section 5.10).

5.1 The right to information

The first right that the data subject can invoke is a request for information about whether, how and why personal data about her are being processed by an organisation. There is no specific exception to this right, so that the data controller must in principle always grant a data subject's request on this point, unless the general exception applies, meaning that either the identity of the data subject cannot be verified or the request is clearly unfounded or excessive.

The data subject is entitled to the following information:
1. The categories of personal data that are processed.
2. The purposes for which the data are used.
3. The organisations with whom the personal data are shared.
4. If the data are transferred to countries outside the EU, the basis on which this is done (section 3.5).
5. Where possible, the retention period (section 3.2).
6. Other rights that the data subject could invoke.
7. Where the personal data are not collected from the data subject directly, information as to the source of the data (see similarly section 4.5).
8. Where applicable, the existence of automated decision-making or profiling activities (section 5.7), including meaningful information about the algorithms involved, as well as the significance and the envisaged consequences of such processing for the data subject.

5.2 The right to access

In addition to the right to information, the data subject has the right to access the data. The data subject should be able to physically or digitally access the part of a particular file or database which contains her personal data.

As with the right to information, there is no specific exception to this right, so that the data controller must in principle always grant a data subject's request on this point, unless the general exception applies, meaning that either the identity of the data subject cannot be verified or the request is clearly unfounded or excessive. What is to be considered a clearly unfounded or excessive access request depends on the context and the specific situation. For example, in a medical context, it is logical that the data subject may want to access her medical file regularly.

More generally, the GDPR encourages organisations to make the personal data and information about the data processing operations permanently accessible to the data subject via online tools or web applications (as part of the general principle of transparency, section 4.4), provided that those tools and applications are safe and secure (sections 4.8 and 4.9).

5.3   The right to copy

The data subject also has the right to a copy of the personal data. For example, a patient may ask to copy her medical file so that she can consult it at home. In addition to the general exception to this right, meaning that the data controller does not have to respect the request from the data subject when either the identity of the data subject cannot be verified or the request is clearly unfounded or excessive, the GDPR specifies that the data controller should not provide a copy of the data when the rights of third parties could be compromised. This may be the case, for instance, when a third party has a copyright or other intellectual property right on the information or when copying the data could jeopardise the privacy and data protection rights of that third party. For example, if the school file of the child of divorced parents suggests that the father may be an alcoholic, such information should in principle be omitted if the mother requests the file on behalf of the child. Importantly, in addition to the general rule that where requests are excessive or clearly unfounded, the data controller may either refuse to comply or charge a reasonable fee for complying with the request, the right to copy is the only right for which data controllers may charge a reasonable fee based on administrative costs.

5.4   The right to data portability

The right to data portability is the equivalent of the right to number portability, also guaranteed by the EU: if a person changes telecom provider, she can keep her phone number. The idea behind the right to data portability is that if you provide data to an organisation such as Facebook, you always have the right to retrieve your personal data and take them to another social network. In essence, this right serves to break the monopoly of large internet companies and to increase competition.

It is unclear how far this right also applies to inferred data. For example, Facebook can make a reasonably good estimate of your gender, age, education, sexual orientation, political preferences, etc., based on your taste in music, friends and likes. Whether these data, which are inferred from the data that have been provided by the data subject, also fall under the right to data portability is unclear and will ultimately be decided by the supervisory authority or a court of law.

The right to data portability applies if two conditions are met:
1. The processing is based on consent (sections 3.3 and 3.4) or a contractual agreement (section 3.3); and
2. The processing should be carried out by automated means, i.e. non-analogue (section 2.2).

If the conditions of this right are met, then the following obligations apply:
1. Provision to data subject: the personal data are in principle transmitted directly to the data subject.
2. Provision to new data controller: if it is technically possible, the data subject may also ask the organisation to send the data directly to the new data controller.
3. Structured and interoperable format: to the extent possible, the data must be provided in a structured, commonly used, machine-readable and interoperable format; that is to say, the new data controller to which the data subject transfers her data must be able to use them in a fairly simple way. What is a commonly used format may differ from sector to sector. Importantly, the right to data portability does not require a data controller to make substantial investments or purchase new systems or technical applications in order to restructure the data in its possession to a commonly used and interoperable format. But when an organisation

buys new software or updates its systems, facilitating data sharing in a structured and interoperable format should be a consideration.

Like the right to copy, in addition to the general exception to this right – the data controller does not have to respect a request from the data subject when either the identity of the data subject cannot be verified or the request is clearly unfounded or excessive – the GDPR specifies that the data controller should not fulfil the data subject's request on this point when the rights of third parties could be compromised.

5.5   The right to rectification and completion

If personal data are incorrect, the data subject may ask for a rectification. In addition, where the data processed by the data controller are incomplete, the data subject has the right to provide supplementary information. It is difficult to determine how broadly this right should be interpreted. A bank might categorise a person as likely to default, but that person might obviously disagree. An employer may use the biological gender of a person, though she may want to be referred to as belonging to a different gender. A person may send the bank additional information, which she thinks should portray her as being trustworthy and creditworthy. But who decides what is correct and what is complete? Ultimately, it is up to a supervisory authority or a court of law to decide on this point, if the data subject and the controller continue to disagree.

As with the right to information and the right to access, there is no specific exception to this right, so the data controller must in principle always fulfil a data subject's request on this point, unless the general exception applies, meaning that either the identity of the data subject cannot be verified or the request is clearly unfounded or excessive.

Importantly, when the data controller does grant the data subject's request, the data controller has to notify all other organisations with which it has shared the incorrect or incomplete data as to how the data should be corrected or supplemented, unless this proves impossible or involves disproportionate effort. The data subject can also ask the data controller for the contact details of these organisations, so that she can verify whether these organisations have also corrected or supplemented the data.

5.6   The right to erasure (right to be forgotten)

The data subject has what is called a right to be forgotten or right to erasure (the official name in the GDPR is the right to erasure, where the right to be forgotten is the nome de plume put behind it between brackets: Right to erasure ('right to be forgotten')), which means she can request that the data controller erase data that are processed in violation with the General Data Protection Regulation.

1. *Background:* the background to this right can be found in three different sources:
   a. First, the idea that a citizen has the right to leave behind a part of her past stems from criminal law. A basic principle of criminal law is that after a criminal has completed her sentence, she can start again with a clean slate. A mistake or bad decision made in the past should not haunt a person for the rest of her life.
   b. Second, before the adoption of the GDPR, the Court of Justice adopted a right to be forgotten in a case that revolved around a man who had gone bankrupt decades before. A newspaper had devoted a small article to it at the time. Subsequently, in the 21st century, the newspaper was digitised, so that the piece was easy to retrieve. After that, Google indexed the newspaper report, showing it as one of the first hits when the name of the man was entered in the search engine. Interestingly, the Court of Justice did not rule that the newspaper violated the data protection framework, either by publishing the

initial report or by digitising it, but found that Google had. Processing these old data and showing them so prominently was considered disproportionate.

   c. Third, the GDPR itself emphasises the protection of children. In particular, there is the fear that children will share photos and videos of themselves and each other without being aware that 'the internet remembers everything'. As the saying goes: what is put online, stays online. The worry is that either children will be haunted by their past, for example when a potential employer finds an online photo of a job applicant on which she is clearly drunk at a party as a teenager, or that children will realise this potential danger and will restrict their behaviour in advance. The GDPR recognises that unbridled experimentation is an important part of the personal development of adolescents and young adults. This includes making stupid mistakes and experimenting with all kinds of things.

2. *Applicability:* Although the right to be forgotten has aura of being a revolutionary and radical doctrine, in fact it is the most mundane and nondescript of all principles in the GDPR. It merely recognises that if the data controller processes personal data in violation of the GDPR, the data subject can request it to stop doing so. The right to erasure or right to be forgotten can be invoked if one of the following conditions applies:

   a. The personal data are no longer necessary for the purposes for which they were collected, meaning that the controller has acted in violation of the Fair Information Principles, specifically the storage limitation principle (section 3.2).

   b. The data subject has withdrawn her consent and there is no other legal ground for processing (sections 3.3 and 3.4).

   c. The data subject has successfully invoked her right to object (section 5.8).

d. The personal data have been processed unlawfully, for example because the purpose limitation principle was not respected.

e. There is a legal obligation to delete the personal data.

f. When a minor has consented to her personal data being processed by an online company or service and she withdraws her consent or the conditions for legitimate consent were not met.

3. *Exceptions:* the controller must in principle grant a data subject's request on this point, unless the general exception applies, meaning that either the identity of the data subject cannot be verified or the request is clearly unfounded or excessive. In addition, the GDPR specifies a number of exceptions that are specific to the right to be forgotten, namely when:

a. Processing of personal data is necessary in order to exercise the right to freedom of expression and information. For example, it may be relevant to know old details of presidential candidates, such as former drug use. The freedom of expression, in such instances, can prevail over the right to be forgotten; or

b. Processing the data is legally required or necessary for the performance of a public task. For example, the police should keep records on former convictions of people; or

c. Data processing is necessary in the context of occupational medicine or public health. This may involve, for example, compromising information about someone who was the source of a gonorrhoea outbreak, where that person would prefer that information be deleted as quickly as possible. Similarly, an employer may keep records about the health of its employers for long periods; or

d. The data are necessary for archiving purposes, scientific research or statistical purposes. If, for example, an archive contains compromising information about a person, she has no right to ask for the data to be deleted; or

e. Processing the personal data is necessary for the establishment, exercise or substantiation of a legal claim.

4. *Notification:* as with the right to rectification, when the data controller does grant the data subject's request, the data controller has to notify all other organisations with which it has shared the data that the data are to be erased, unless this proves impossible or involves disproportionate effort. The data subject can also ask the data controller for the contact details of these organisations, so that she can verify whether they have also erased the data. Importantly, an additional principle applies, which is only recognised vis-à-vis the right to erasure, namely that when the data controller has made the data public, for example on the internet, it has the obligation to take all reasonable steps possible to inform all other persons and organisations that are processing such personal data (for example having copied a video, photo or text message and published it on another website) of the fact that they have to erase any links to or copies or replications of those personal data.

5.7 The right not to be subject to automated decision-making

The data controller has the duty not to subject a person to automated decisions without human intervention, i.e. computer models and algorithms that make independent decisions, if those decisions have a major impact on the data subject's life. Automated decision-making is often based on profiling, through which personal data are used to evaluate personal aspects of an individual's life, such as performance at work, economic situation, health, personal preferences, interests, reliability, behaviour, location or movements.

1. *Background:* computer programs and algorithms often work on the basis of general patterns and rules, such as: 70% of people with curly hair would be interested in a certain type of shampoo; 30% of people with a university degree that live in the 9th arrondissement of Paris are opera lovers; 5% of men

between 20 and 30 years old who have recently obtained a car will be involved in a car incident. Such general patterns can be used to make decisions, for example, which group to show an advertisement, which group can be offered a discount or which group may be eligible for a car insurance and under what conditions. The General Data Protection Regulation requires that, when such a decision has a substantial impact on a person, there should always be a human in the decision-making loop. For example, although it may be true that a higher percentage of men with grey hair repay their loan than men with other hair colours, a bank cannot have an algorithm decide whether or not to give a man a loan based on his hair colour. A human employee should always assess whether the general profile also applies to the specific case in hand, taking into account the specific circumstance, the individual background of the person and the particularities of the context.

2. *Conditions:* the obligation not to subject people to automated decisions without human intervention is subject to two cummulative conditions.

    a. The prohibition only applies to decisions based 'solely' on automated processing. What should be the level of involvement of a human to qualify a decision as not being based 'solely' on automated processing is not specified by the GDPR. It will not be enough to say that, for example, a human has developed the algorithm and that a human was thus involved in the decision-making process. But if an algorithm makes the initial decision, which is assessed and confirmed by a human, this may be sufficient for GDPR compliance on this point.

    b. The decision should have a legal effect or significantly affect a person. The threshold is not specified by the GDPR. In general, advertisements shown on the basis of profiling will not be considered to have a significant effect on a person, but selecting candidates for a job interview will.

3. *Exceptions for automated decision-making based on non-sensitive personal data:* if these two conditions are met, the prohibition on automated decision-making applies, unless additional protection is provided to the interests of the data subjects involved and one of the following three grounds applies:
   a. The automated decision-making is explicitly permitted by EU or national law (for the conditions, see section 3.3). On this point, the GDPR gives as example automated decision-making for fraud and tax-evasion monitoring. Another example may be speeding fines that are processed automatically.
   b. The automated decision-making is necessary for the establishment or implementation of an agreement between the data subject and the controller (for the conditions, see section 3.3);
   c. The automated decision-making is based on the explicit consent of the data subject (for the conditions, see sections 3.3 and 3.4).
4. *Exceptions for automated decision-making based on sensitive personal data*: for automated decision-making on the basis of sensitive personal data, the prohibition on automated decision-making applies when the two conditions have been met, unless additional protection is provided to the interests of the data subjects involved and one of the following two grounds applies:
   a. The data subject has given explicit consent (section 3.4: for the conditions, see sections 3.3 and 3.4).
   b. It is necessary due to a substantial public interest (section 3.4).

5.8   The right to object

1. *Background:* the background of the right to object is twofold:
   a. In part, this right aims to restrict personalised advertisements on the internet. Personal data are collected and

personalised advertisements are displayed based on these data. In a sense, the right to object is the mirror of the prohibition on automatic decision-making. That prohibition applies to decisions that have a substantial impact on the data subject. The right to object applies, in part, to profiling which has a minor effect on the data subject. While the provision on automated decision-making is phrased mainly as a duty of the data controller, the right to object is a subjective right of the data subject. The data controller can offer personalised advertisements, unless the data subject objects.

b. For another part, this right applies to all processing operations that are based either on the legitimate interest of the data controller, which overrides the interests of the data subject, or on a public interest or task (two of the six processing grounds discussed in section 3.3). The data subject can, by virtue of her right to object, challenge whether the data controller is indeed processing personal data that are necessary in light of a public interest or has an interest that overrides the interests of the data subject. Because these are ultimately subjective interpretations, the GDPR allows the data subject to present arguments to the contrary. When the data controller and the data subject continue to disagree, it is ultimately up to the supervisory authority or judge to decide on the matter.

2. *Applicability:* this right only applies if two conditions both apply:

a. The request concerns the specific case of the data subject alone. For example, Mr Brown may indicate that he no longer wants to be profiled by a particular organisation. But the right to object does not give him the right to ask an organisation to stop profiling altogether. Mr Brown can argue that in his specific case, data processing does not serve a public interest or that in his case, his interests override those of the data controller, but he cannot generally object to the controller invoking one of the two legal grounds for legitimate processing.

    b.   The right to object can only be invoked if:

        i.   The data subject's claim concerns direct marketing activities; or

        ii.   The legal ground for processing (section 3.3) that is invoked is:

            1.   The public interest or the performance of a public task; or

            2.   The legitimate interests of the controller.

3.   *Exceptions:* the data controller does not have to fulfil the data subject's requests if it cannot establish the identity of the data subject or when the request is excessive or clearly unfounded. In addition, the GDPR specifies that the data controller may deny the data subject's request if the data are not used for direct marketing purposes and:

    a.   The controller gives compelling legitimate grounds for the processing which override the interests, rights and freedoms of the data subject, being either its own interests or the public interest. This exception applies to, for example, the national archive or a university processing data in the public interest; or

    b.   Processing the personal data is necessary for the institution, exercise or substantiation of a legal claim.

5.9   The right to restrict

The data subject can also request that the data controller stop processing her personal data. This concerns all processing activities (see section 2.2 for a description), except for storing the data. Consequently, the data controller can keep the personal data in its possession, but cannot use them in any way.

1.   *Background:* the right of restriction is a subsidiary right, which the data subject will invoke after having invoked one of her other rights. For example, when the data subject invokes

her right to rectification, she may additionally invoke her right to restrict, through which she asks the data controller to stop using her data until it has rectified the personal data.

2. *Applicability:* there are four cases in which the data subject can legitimately invoke this right:

   a. The data subject invokes her right to rectification or completion (section 5.5). As explained above, a typical example may be the situation in which the data subject requests that the data controller stop using her data until it has rectified or completed them.

   b. The data subject has invoked her right to object (section 5.8). When the data subject questions whether the data controller has a legal ground for processing her personal data, she may request that the data controller stop using her data until it has verified that it has a legal basis for processing.

   c. If the personal data are processed contrary to the GDPR, the data subject can invoke her right to restrict. For example, if the data controller has no legitimate ground for processing (section 3.3), it should in principle delete the data. But if the data subject wants the data controller to process the personal data legitimately, she can invoke her right to restrict, thus giving the data controller time to find a legitimate ground for processing, without having to delete the data.

   d. The data controller no longer needs to process the personal data, but the data subject needs the data for filing a complaint (section 5.10). This can be the case, for example, when the data subject needs the data in order to show that the data controller has not kept them up to date.

3. *Exceptions:* the data controller does not have to grant the data subject's requests if it cannot establish the data subject's identity or if the request is excessive or clearly unfounded. In addition, the GDPR specifies that the data controller can deny the data subject's request if one of the following situations applies:

a. The data subject agrees with the processing of her personal data. For example, the data controller can ask whether it can still send her a newsletter, while the data are restricted.

b. The data controller needs to process the personal data for the exercise or defence of legal claims. For example, when a data subject has issued a complaint against the data controller, the data controller can use the data to argue, for example, that the data were not incorrect or out of date.

c. To protect the rights of other people or organisations. For example, if a file relates to a mother and a father, and the mother has invoked her right to restrict and uses the data for issuing a complaint against the father, the organisation may still provide the data to the father if he wants to use them for the court case.

d. To protect important reasons of public interest. If the personal data, for example, disclose the fact that a person is suffering from a contagious disease, the medical institution will rely on the public interest for processing such data. However, a data subject has the right to object (section 5.8), arguing that it is not in the public interest, and subsequently invoke her right to restrict. In such a situation, the medical institution may still process the information or share it with competent authorities.

4. *Information:* if the data controller has granted a data subject's right to restrict and it plans to lift the restriction at a later date, it must inform the data subject before using her personal data. For example, if the data subject has invoked her right to restrict because the data were incorrect, the data controller has the right to inform the data subject that it will start using her data again when it has corrected them. This gives the data subject the opportunity to object and argue that the data are still incorrect.

5. *Notification:* as with the right to rectification and the right to be forgotten, when the data controller grants the data

subject's request, it has to notify all the other organisations with which it has shared the data that the data have been restricted, unless this proves impossible or involves disproportionate effort. The data subject can also ask the data controller for the contact details of these organisations, so that she can verify herself whether these organisations have also restricted the data.

5.10   The right to file a complaint

Finally, data subjects may always file a complaint with the national supervisory authority or a court of law. The data subject can go to the supervisory authority or the court if she believes a data controller or processor has violated the GDPR. In addition, she can go to court if she believes the supervisory authority did not act appropriately. For example, if she has filed a complaint about a data controller or processor, but the supervisory authority has rejected her complaint because an investigation found the complaint to be unfounded, the data subject may challenge that decision in court. She can also challenge a decision taken by the European Data Protection Board (EDPB) before the Court of Justice.

The GDPR allows Member States to embed in their legal system the possibility that, when a data subject makes a complaint, she can be represented by civil rights organisations. In addition, Member States can allow such organisations to take legal action on behalf of the data subject, either at her explicit request or when she does not explicitly object to such a procedure. As explained in Chapter 1, in the current data-driven environment there are so many data gathered about a data subject by so many different organisations that it is unrealistic to expect a data subject to assess the legal validity of all these processes and, if she suspects a GDPR violation, to go to court. That is why the GDPR allows specialised organisations to monitor GDPR compliance on their behalf. It is important for these to be not-for-profit organisations;

the GDPR does not want to promote a claim culture based on financial interests. Although the administrative fines can be high, European courts typically do not award high sums to victims of fundamental rights violations. Rather, most requests by data subjects to a court of law will regard stopping, blocking or limiting future data processing activities by data controllers or processors.

5.11   Conclusion

This chapter has discussed the rights of the data subject. The majority of rights directly correlate with the duties of the data controller discussed earlier in this book.

When dealing with requests from data subjects, the data controller should respond swiftly and use clear and understandable language. Preferably, the data controller should allow the data subject to make requests digitally.

Some rights have specific exceptions, such as the right to erasure (right to be forgotten), which does not have to be granted if processing the personal data is necessary for freedom of expression. In addition, the GDPR recognises two general exceptions. If the data controller cannot establish the identity of the data subject, it may refuse to fulfil her request. If the data subject's requests are repetitive or clearly unfounded, the data controller may decide not to grant her requests or to ask for reasonable remuneration.

If a request from the data subject – invoking her right to rectification, to be forgotten or to limitation – is granted, the data controller has to ensure that all other parties to which the data have been transferred are informed of that fact. In the case of the right to be forgotten, or right to erasure, this obligation extends to anyone that has copied the data when they were published on the internet.

Information	Access	Copy	Data portability	Rectification
A data subject has the right to information on the data that are being processed about her, such as: – Categories of personal data being processed; and – Purposes of processing; and – Organisations with whom the data are shared; and – If the data are transferred to non-EU territory, which ground applies; and – Retention period; and – Other data subject rights; and – Information as to the source of the data; and – Where applicable, the existence of automated decision-making.	A data subject has the right to access the data that are being processed about her, preferably in digital and permanent form;	A data subject has the right to a copy of the data that are being processed about her, preferably in digital and continuous form;	A data subject has the right to be sent her data or have the data controller send her personal data to a new data controller, preferably in a structured and interoperable format;	A data subject has the right to have her personal data rectified or completed by the data controller; and
				Have the data controller forward her request to the organisations with whom the data controller has shared the data;

Information	Access	Copy	Data portability	Rectification
Unless her identity cannot be established or her request is clearly unfounded or repetitive.	Unless her identity cannot be established or her request is clearly unfounded or repetitive.	On condition that she pays a reasonable fee based on administrative costs when so required by the data controller;	On condition that: – The data are automatically processed; and – The legal ground used by the data controller is consent or contract;	
		Unless her identity cannot be established or her request is clearly unfounded or repetitive; or	Unless her identity cannot be established or her request is clearly unfounded or repetitive; or	Unless her identity cannot be established or her request is clearly unfounded or repetitive; or
		Unless it would undermine the rights of third parties.	Unless it would undermine the rights of third parties.	Unless, with respect to the right to have the request forwarded, this proves impossible or involves disproportionate effort.

Erasure (Forgotten)	Automated decision-making	Object	Restrict	Complaint
A data subject has the right to erase her personal data; and	A data subject has the right not to be subject to automated decision-making;	A data subject has the right to object to processing personal data in her specific individual case;	A data subject has the right to request that a data controller stop processing her data, except for storing them; and	A data subject may file a complaint with the national supervisory authority about a person or organisation that has violated the GDPR; and
Have the data controller forward her request to the organisations with whom the data controller has shared the data; and			Have the data controller inform her before using her data again after they have been restricted; and	A data subject may file a complaint with a court of law about a person or organisation that has violated the GDPR or about a decision taken by the supervisory authority; and
Have the data controller inform other parties that process her data of her request when the controller has made the personal data public, for example by publishing them on the internet;			Have the data controller forward her request to the organisations with whom the data controller has shared the data;	A data subject can be represented in her claims by civil society organisations;
On condition that data processing is not GDPR-compliant, such as when: - Data processing is no longer necessary; or - The data controller no longer has a legitimate ground for processing the data; or - There is a legal obligation to delete the data.	On condition that the decision-making is: - Solely based on automated processing; and - The decision has a significant effect on the data subject;	On condition that: - Her claim concerns direct marketing activities; or - The legal ground for processing that is invoked by the data controller is: • The public interest or the performance of a public task; or • The legitimate interests of the controller;	On condition that: - The data subject has also invoked her right to rectification; or - The data subject has also invoked her right to object; or - The personal data are processed contrary to the GDPR; or - Processing the personal data is no longer necessary for the data controller, but the data subject needs the data for filing a complaint;	

Erasure (Forgotten)	Automated decision-making	Object	Restrict	Complaint
Unless her identity cannot be established or her request is clearly unfounded or repetitive; or Unless personal data are necessary for: – freedom of expression; or – for a legal obligation; or – for occupational medicine or public health; or – for archiving purposes, scientific research or statistical purposes; or – for the establishment, exercise or substantiation of a legal claim Or; Unless, with respect to the right to have the request forwarded, this proves impossible or involves disproportionate effort.	Unless her identity cannot be established or her request is clearly unfounded or repetitive; or Unless, in the case of automated decision-making based on personal data, this is based on: – A law; or – Explicit consent; or – Contract; Or; Unless, in the case of automated decision-making based on sensitive personal data, this is based on: – Explicit consent; or – A substantial public interest.	Unless her identity cannot be established or her request is clearly unfounded or repetitive; or Unless – The controller demonstrates that either its own interests or the public interest overrides the interests of the data subject; or – Processing the personal data is necessary for the institution, exercise or substantiation of a legal claim.	Unless her identity cannot be established or her request is clearly unfounded or repetitive; or Unless – The data subject agrees with the processing of her personal data for specified purposes; or – The data controller needs to process the personal data for the exercise or defence of a legal claim; or – Data processing is necessary to protect the rights of other persons or organisations; or – Data processing is necessary to protect important reasons of public interest. Or; Unless, with respect to the right to have the request forwarded, this proves impossible or involves disproportionate effort.	Unless her identity cannot be established or her request is clearly unfounded or repetitive.

6. How is the GDPR monitored and enforced?

This final chapter will explain how the GDPR is applied in practice, which additional guidelines and codes can be adopted and how potential violations of the data protection framework are monitored and sanctioned.

It will discuss two forms of self-regulation: codes of conduct (section 6.1) and certification mechanisms (section 6.2). It will explain which bodies are granted regulatory powers by the GDPR and what competences they have. These are the national supervisory authority (section 6.3), the lead authority (section 6.4), the European Data Protection Board (section 6.5) and the European Commission (section 6.6). These organs have the authority to issue guidelines on the correct interpretation and implementation of the rules in practice. They also have the power to monitor and enforce the data protection framework.

The chapter also briefly highlights two other important sources for the data protection framework, namely the national laws implementing the GDPR on the points where Member States are allowed discretion (section 6.7) and judgments by the courts, having the final say on the correct interpretation and application of the GDPR (section 6.8).

Finally, the chapter will discuss two of the most important consequences of violating the data protection framework: either a national supervisory authority can impose sanctions and fines (section 6.9) or a court can impose sanctions on data controllers and processors, and award damages to data subjects (section 6.10).

6.1   Codes of conduct

The GDPR leaves room for two forms of self-regulation.

First, codes of conduct can be adopted by branch organisations or representative bodies (discussed in this section). If such a body adopts a code of conduct, all its member organisations must comply with the code. Thus, although a branch organisation or representative body does not have to adopt a code of conduct, when it is adopted, it has binding force.

Second, an organisation can apply for a certificate, such as a certificate showing that the organisation has taken adequate technical and organisational security measures (discussed in section 6.2). If such a certificate is available, organisations are in no way obliged to obtain it.

Codes of conduct already existed under the Data Protection Directive from 1995 and they will be adopted under the GDPR both at national and EU-wide level. Codes of conduct having an effect at national level have to be approved by the national supervisory authority, while the EU-wide codes of conduct have to be approved by the European Data Protection Board.

A code of conduct enables a particular sector to specify in further detail how the rules in the GDPR will be explained and interpreted in its case. For example, the representative organ of the national universities can propose to the national supervisory authority a code of conduct for its sector. This code will explain in further detail how the general principles and obligations in the GDPR will be followed by the national universities and provide further guidance on the conditions under which and the extent to which the various exceptions provided in the GDPR for data processing for scientific research purposes can be invoked by academic researchers.

The GDPR suggests that such a code of conduct can give further specifications on points such as, but not limited to:
- fair and transparent processing;
- the legitimate interests pursued by controllers in specific contexts;
- the collection of personal data;
- the pseudonymisation of personal data;
- the information provided to the public and to data subjects;
- the exercise of the rights of data subjects;

- the information provided to, and the protection of, children, and the manner in which parental consent is to be obtained;
- technical and organisational (security) measures to ensure compliance with the GDPR;
- the notification of personal data breaches to supervisory authorities and to data subjects;
- the transfer of personal data to third countries or international organisations; and
- out-of-court proceedings and other dispute resolution procedures for resolving disputes between controllers and data subjects.

Importantly, not only data controllers and processors that are themselves bound by the GDPR, but also non-EU-based organisations with whom EU-based organisations share data can subject themselves to such a code of conduct (section 2.3). When they do so and the code has been approved by the national supervisory authority or the EDPB, and the European Commission has also approved the code of conduct, the code will be seen as a legal document that guarantees adequate safeguards, so that transfer of personal data to these organisations will be considered legitimate (section 3.5).

A code of conduct may also install a body to oversee the application and enforcement of the document. Such a body can take over some of the tasks and responsibilities of the national supervisory authority or EDPB relating to monitoring and enforcing the data protection framework, although the national supervisory authority and the EDPB always retain their powers and competences and also oversee the accreditation of the body installed by the code. The GDPR specifies that before being accredited by the national supervisory authority or EDPB, such a body must have:
- demonstrated its independence and expertise in relation to the subject matter of the code; and
- established procedures which allow it to assess the eligibility of controllers and processors concerned with applying the code, to monitor their compliance with the code and to review the code periodically; and

- established procedures and structures to handle complaints about infringements of the code or the manner in which the code is being implemented by a controller or processor, and to make those procedures and structures transparent to data subjects and the public; and
- demonstrated that its tasks and duties do not result in a conflict of interest.

6.2 Certification mechanisms

A second form of self-regulation is certification. In brief, certificates are proof that an organisation is GDPR-compliant on a particular point, for example that it has taken adequate organisational and technical security measures. There is discussion about the extent to which a certificate may be provided for GDPR compliance in general; on this point, the EDPB is expected to provide further clarity in the near future.

Certificates can be issued by official certification bodies, which in turn must be accredited by the national supervisory authority or a national accreditation organisation. For cross-border data processing, the EDPB shall have authority.

A certification body will only be accredited if it has sufficient expertise and resources to carry out its task properly, if it is independent and if there is no conflict of interest. For example, a company may not sell certificates to organisations without properly checking whether the requirements for giving the certificate have indeed been met and continue to be met. The certification body should be objective, independent and neutral, and must be transparent. It should have a procedure for complaints for when organisations do not comply with the conditions applicable to the certificate. The certification body should do periodic reviews of the organisations that have been granted a certificate and establish procedures for withdrawing certification.

Certificates can be issued to a controller or processor for a maximum of three years, but may be renewed, of course provided that the relevant requirements continue to be met.

The supervisory authority or national accreditation body accrediting the certification body must oversee that body. The accreditation of a certification body can be issued for a maximum period of five years, but may be renewed provided the certification body continues to meet the requirements.

6.3   The national supervisory authority

The GDPR mentions 22 specific tasks and 26 specific powers that national supervisory organisations have.

In general, six types of task can be distinguished:
1. Teacher: the supervisory authority should increase the general awareness of data protection law among the public by providing information and facilitating education;
2. Adviser: the supervisory authority can advise organisations on how to implement the various aspects of the GDPR within an organisation, such as with regard to doing an impact assessment, and can advise the national legislator, when adopting a law in the field of data protection;
3. Regulator: the supervisory authority can itself adopt regulations and standards, such as standard contractual clauses for transferring personal data to a non-EU territory (section 3.5), laying down the requirements for impact assessments (section 4.6) and setting out the criteria for accreditation (sections 6.1 and 6.2);
4. Ombudsman: the supervisory authority can deal with specific complaints about specific situations that it has received from data subjects;
5. Supervisor: one of the main tasks of the supervisory authority is overseeing the application and implementation of the Regulation. To that end, it monitors the relevant developments in

the field of data protection, both in general and with respect to specific sectors and organisations; and

6. Sanctioning body: the supervisory authority can impose sanctions and fines when it establishes a violation. It also has the power to bring infringements of the GDPR to the attention of the judicial authorities and to commence legal proceedings in order to enforce the provisions of the GDPR.

The 26 powers of the supervisory authority can be used in relation to both the data controller and the data processor and can be subdivided into powers relating to advice, investigation and sanctions.

1. The investigative powers include the power:
   a. to order an organisation to provide any information it requires for the performance of its tasks;
   b. to carry out data protection audits;
   c. to carry out a review on certifications;
   d. to notify an organisation of an alleged infringement;
   e. to obtain access to all personal data and to all information necessary; and
   f. to obtain access to any premises of an organisation, including to any data processing equipment and means.
2. The corrective powers include the power:
   a. to issue warnings that intended processing operations are likely to infringe the GDPR;
   b. to issue reprimands where processing operations have infringed the GDPR;
   c. to order an organisation to comply with a data subject's request (Chapter 5);
   d. to order an organisation to bring processing operations into compliance with the GDPR, in a specified manner and within a specified time frame;
   e. to order the controller to inform data subjects of a personal data breach (section 4.10);
   f. to impose a temporary or definitive limitation, including a ban on processing;

g. to order the rectification, erasure or restriction of personal data and the notification of such actions to recipients to whom the personal data have been disclosed (sections 5.5, 5.6 and 5.9);

h. to withdraw a certificate or to order the certification body to withdraw a certificate (section 6.2);

i. to impose an administrative fine (section 6.9); and

j. to order the suspension of data flows to a recipient in a non-EU country (section 3.5).

3. The advisory powers include the power:

a. to advise the controller on risky data processing operations (section 4.6);

b. to issue opinions to the national parliament and the national government on any issue related to the protection of personal data;

c. to authorise processing operations in the public interest if the law of the Member State requires such prior authorisation;

d. to issue an opinion on and approve draft codes of conduct (section 6.1);

e. to accredit certification bodies (section 6.2);

f. to issue certificates and approve certification criteria (section 6.2);

g. to adopt standard data protection clauses (section 3.5);

h. to authorise contractual clauses (section 3.5);

i. to authorise administrative arrangements (section 3.5); and

j. to approve binding corporate rules (section 3.5).

Data controllers and processors must check regularly whether the supervisory authority has issued new guidelines or principles that are relevant to them. An organisation has to comply with the orders of the supervisory authority. It can go to court if it disagrees with a decision or sanction.

Supervisory authorities are not competent to supervise processing operations of courts acting in their judicial capacity.

Member States must at least appoint one national supervisory authority, but may also install more than one authority, for example installing a separate authority per province or state or a separate authority for specific sectors, such as a data protection authority for the medical or the telecom sector.

Each national supervisory authority should be completely independent in performing its tasks and exercising its powers. The board of each supervisory authority cannot receive instructions from anybody, such as the government, the president or members of parliament. In addition, the board of the supervisory authority cannot have other functions, ties or connections that could lead to a conflict of interest. Although the board members are appointed by either parliament, the government, the head of state or an independent body entrusted with this task, the GDPR specifies that they have to be selected on the basis of their qualifications, experience and skills. Member States have the obligation to ensure that each supervisory authority is provided with the human, technical and financial resources, premises and infrastructure necessary for performing its tasks and exercising its powers effectively and that it has its own staff, subject to the exclusive direction of the board of the supervisory authority.

In the past, the European Court of Justice has on multiple occasions found a violation of the data protection framework because Member States had insufficiently guaranteed the independence of their national supervisory authority.

6.4   The lead supervisory authority

The General Data Protection Regulation stipulates that the various national supervisory organisations in the EU should cooperate with respect to cross-border data processing operations and in scrutinising companies located or operating in multiple EU countries. They should assist each other, for example by giving advice, sharing information and providing mutual assistance. If, for instance, a company operates in Poland, Hungary and Malta, then the Polish, Hungarian and Maltese national supervisory authorities are 'supervisory authorities concerned', which in principle have competence to oversee the processing operations of this company.

To avoid the supervisory authorities concerned duplicating work and to avoid potentially conflicting requirements and obligations being imposed by two or more supervisory authorities on one data controller or processor, the GDPR specifies that a 'lead supervisory authority' can be selected from these supervisory authorities concerned. The lead supervisory authority, as the name suggests, takes the lead in overseeing the data processing operations and enforcing the GDPR with respect to that company. The lead supervisory authority has all the powers and competences a national supervisory authority normally has (section 6.3).

The other supervisory authorities concerned should follow its instructions and execute the decisions it takes. The lead supervisory authority has the obligation to consult with the other supervisory authorities concerned before making a decision, but it has the ultimate power to decide on the course taken. If one of the other supervisory authorities concerned disagrees with a decision taken by the lead supervisory authority, it can submit a complaint to the European Data Protection Board, which can decide on the matter.

A lead supervisory authority will be appointed in the case of cross-border data processing, which is the situation in which one organisation is either established in more than one Member State and engages in data processing activities, or is established in one Member State, but its processing operations also concern and substantially affect citizens of other EU Member States.

The lead supervisory authority will be the authority where the organisation has its main establishment. If an organisation has one establishment, this will be the supervisory authority on whose territory the organisation is located. If an organisation has establishments in more than one Member State, this will be the place of its central administration in the EU.

The GDPR specifies two exceptions to the appointment of a lead supervisory authority:

1. Each supervisory authority will be competent to handle a complaint lodged with it by a data subject if the subject matter relates only to an establishment in its Member State or substantially affects data subjects only in its Member State. For example, if a company operates in both Ireland and Lithuania and has its main establishment in Ireland, and a data subject submits a complaint to the Lithuanian supervisory authority with respect to a behavioural advertising campaign by that company directed specifically at Lithuanian citizens, the Lithuanian supervisory authority will be competent to handle the complaint, even though the Irish supervisory authority may be the lead supervisory authority.

2. Where processing is carried out by public authorities or private bodies acting on the basis of a legal obligation or a public interest or task (section 3.3). Suppose the Czech government has hired a Slovakian private security organisation to help maintain public order during international football matches. In such a case, the Slovakian organisation, which has its main establishment in Slovakia, may process the personal data of many EU citizens that it helps identify and arrest. However, the Czech supervisory authority will be competent to oversee the data processing operations of the Slovakian company performed for the purpose of maintaining public order in the Czech Republic.

6.5   The European Data Protection Board

The European Data Protection Board (EDPB) replaces the Article 29 Working Party, which was put in place by the Data Protection Directive from 1995. The Article 29 Working Party issued opinions on the interpretation of the various rights, obligations and principles contained in the Directive. Because all national supervisory authorities were represented in the

Working Party, these recommendations were very influential. The European Data Protection Board will continue on this path and has more powers and competences than the Article 29 Working Party had.

Each EU Member State has one representative in the Board. Member States are allowed to install more than one national supervisory authority (section 6.3). In such a case, the Member State should make one of the national supervisory authorities the main supervisory authority. This will typically be the nationwide, general data protection authority. The main supervisory authority has the right to send a representative to the EDPB, but it should also consult with and represent the interests of the other national supervisory authorities. The vote of each of the 28 members has equal weight; decisions are typically taken by simple majority.

As well as the representatives of each Member State, the European Data Protection Supervisor has one seat in the EDPB. The European Data Protection Supervisor is the supervisory authority overseeing data processing operations by EU institutions themselves, such as the European Central Bank, the European Economic and Social Committee, the European Investment Bank and the European Ombudsman. The GDPR does not apply to the processing of personal data by EU institutions, but a separate regulation does. The European Data Protection Supervisor has voting rights only on decisions concerning principles and rules in the GDPR that correspond to those contained in the separate regulation for data processing by EU institutions (section 2.4).

The tasks and powers of the EDPB can be roughly divided into four categories:

1. It can issue opinions and guidelines on the various aspects of the GDPR;
2. It can issue and scrutinise EU-wide codes of conduct and certification mechanisms and sanction transnational data flows;
3. It can advise various organs, such as the European Commission and the European Parliament on data protection related aspects; and

4. It can act as a dispute resolution mechanism when supervisory authorities concerned disagree with decisions taken by the lead supervisory authority.

The GDPR distinguishes no fewer than 25 official tasks, which are to a large extent similar to the tasks of the national supervisory authorities:

1. monitoring and ensuring the correct application of the GDPR;
2. issuing guidelines, recommendations and best practices in order to encourage consistent application of the GDPR;
3. issuing guidelines, recommendations and best practices further specifying the criteria and requirements for data transfers based on binding corporate rules (section 3.5);
4. issuing guidelines, recommendations and best practices further specifying the criteria and requirements for incidental data transfers based on grounds such as consent, contract and the public interest (section 3.5);
5. issuing guidelines, recommendations and best practices for establishing data breaches and the undue delay for data breach notifications (section 4.10);
6. issuing guidelines, recommendations and best practices as to the circumstances in which a personal data breach is likely to result in a high risk (section 4.10);
7. issuing guidelines, recommendations and best practices on procedures for erasing links, copies or replications of personal data that should be erased from publicly available communication services (section 5.6);
8. issuing guidelines, recommendations and best practices further specifying the criteria and conditions for decisions based on profiling (section 5.7);
9. issuing guidelines, recommendations and best practices for establishing common procedures for reporting by natural persons of infringements to staff members of the national supervisory authority who are under a duty of professional secrecy (section 6.3);

10. drawing up guidelines for supervisory authorities concerning the application of measures and setting administrative fines (sections 6.3 and 6.9);
11. reviewing the practical application of the guidelines, recommendations and best practices;
12. issuing opinions on draft decisions of supervisory authorities in case of cross-border data processing and multiple supervisory authorities concerned (section 6.3);
13. issuing opinions on codes of conduct drawn up at Union level (section 6.1);
14. advising the Commission on any issue related to the protection of personal data, including any proposed amendment of the GDPR;
15. advising the Commission on the format and procedures for the exchange of information between controllers, processors and supervisory authorities for binding corporate rules;
16. providing the Commission with an opinion on the certification requirements (section 6.2);
17. providing the Commission with an opinion on icons (section 6.6);
18. providing the Commission with an opinion on the assessment of the adequacy of the level of protection in a third country (section 3.5);
19. encouraging the drawing-up of codes of conduct and the establishment of data protection certification mechanisms (sections 6.1 and 6.2);
20. carrying out the accreditation of certification bodies and its periodic review and maintaining a public register of accredited bodies and of the accredited controllers or processors established in third countries (section 6.2);
21. specifying the requirements with a view to the accreditation of certification bodies (section 6.2);
22. promoting the cooperation and the effective bilateral and multilateral exchange of information and best practices between the supervisory authorities;

23. promoting common training programmes and facilitating personnel exchanges between the supervisory authorities;
24. promoting the exchange of knowledge and documentation on data protection legislation and practice with data protection supervisory authorities worldwide; and
25. maintaining a publicly accessible electronic register of decisions taken by supervisory authorities and courts on issues relating to cross-border data processing and data processing matters with multiple supervisory authorities concerned.

Like the national supervisory authority, the EDPB should be and act fully independently.

6.6   The European Commission

The European Commission can be compared to the government (executive power) of the European Union. Its Commissioners can be compared to ministers acting at EU level. There is a Commissioner of Trade, a Commissioner of Transport, a Commissioner of Economic and Financial affairs, a Commissioner of Competition, a Commissioner of Justice, a Commissioner of Security, and so forth.

The GDPR grants the Commission competences and powers on several points:

1. As explained in section 3.5, it can adopt adequacy decisions, which allow personal data to be transferred to a non-EU country as if it were an EU country, because the non-EU country guarantees a level of data protection that is equivalent to the GDPR, through its national legal system.
2. The Commission can approve standard contractual clauses on several points. It can adopt standard contractual clauses for the legal relationship between data controller and data processor and between data processor and sub-processor (section 2.5). It can also adopt standard contractual clauses providing appropriate safeguards and a basis on which an

EU-based organisation and a non-EU-based organisation can legitimately share personal data (section 3.5).

3. National supervisory authorities can also adopt standard contractual clauses for transferring personal data to non-EU-based organisations (section 3.5), but those need to be approved by the Commission.

4. Both the Commission and supervisory authorities can take appropriate steps to promote international cooperation mechanisms to help ensure that data protection legislation is effectively enforced, to provide international mutual assistance in enforcing the legislation, to engage in activities aimed at furthering international cooperation in enforcing legislation, and to promote the exchange and documentation of personal data protection legislation and practice.

5. When a code of conduct is approved by the national supervisory authority or the EDPB, the Commission may decide that the code is generally valid within the EU. Controllers or processors that are not subject to the GDPR may also adhere to such a code; as such, it may provide a legal agreement that gives appropriate safeguards for transferring personal data to these non-EU-based organisations (section 3.5).

6. The Commission has the power to specify the requirements to be taken into account for the data protection certification mechanisms and it may lay down technical standards for certification mechanisms and mechanisms to promote and recognise those certification mechanisms. It is also empowered to give further guidance and to take the initiative for an EU certification mechanism (section 6.2).

7. The Commission may specify the format and procedures for information exchanges between controllers, processors and supervisory authorities for binding corporate rules (section 3.5) as well as for mutual assistance and the exchange of information by electronic means between supervisory authorities, and between supervisory authorities and the EDPB, in particular the standardised format (sections 6.4 and 6.5).

8. The Commission may request that any matter of general application or producing effects in more than one Member State be examined by the EDPB with a view to obtaining an opinion, in particular where a competent supervisory authority does not comply with the obligations for mutual assistance.

9. The Commission has the right to participate in the activities and meetings of the Board without voting rights. The Commission may also ask the EDPB to perform one of its tasks, within a specified time limit.

10. The Commission is empowered to give further guidance on the way in which the data controller should communicate with the data subject, particularly regarding the obligation of transparency and information and the requests that the data subject makes when invoking one of her rights (sections 4.4 and 4.5, Chapter 5). This could be done by developing icons. Such icons or labels have already been developed in other sectors, for example for the energy market. In an earlier version of the GDPR (which was not adopted), a first attempt was made to arrive at such standardised icons (shown on the next page). The European Commission is expected to develop concrete proposals for developing icons that can be used to inform the data subject simply and clearly about which data are processed, how and for which purposes.

11. The Commission should be notified of important decisions taken by Member States, the national supervisory authority and the EDPB. For example, the GDPR specifies that Member States may decide that data controllers need the prior approval of the national supervisory authority when they want to process personal data based on the public interest and that Member States may decide that occasional data transfers for important reasons of public interests can be limited. The Commission should be informed of such legal provisions. Member States also need to inform the Commission about laws they adopt in which they lay down the powers and competences of national supervisory authorities. Where the legal system of

	No personal data are **collected** beyond the minimum necessary for each specific purpose of the processing	✓
	No personal data are **retained** beyond the minimum necessary for each specific purpose of the processing	✓
	No personal data are **processed** for purposes other than the purposes for which they were collected	✓
	No personal data are **disseminated** to non-public third parties for purposes other than the purposes for which they were collected	✓
	No personal data are **sold**	✓
	No personal data are retained in **unencrypted** form	X

the Member State does not provide for administrative fines (for example leaving it to a court of law to decide on such sanctions), Member States have to notify the Commission of such provisions in their legislation. The GDPR specifies that Member States have to lay down the rules for penalties other than administrative fines that can be imposed for infringements of the GDPR, in particular for those that are not subject to administrative fines. Again, Member States have to notify the Commission of the legal provisions it adopts. When Member States impose limitations on specific parts of the GDPR because it is thought necessary for freedom of speech, in the context of employment or for the protection of professional secrecy, it has the obligation to inform the Commission. In another example, when the EDPB acts as dispute resolution organ for conflicts between supervisory authorities concerned, it should inform the Commission of its decisions. The Board must also forward its opinions, guidelines and recommendations to the Commission. The Board and all national supervisory authorities have to draw up an annual report and send it to the Commission, among others.

12. The Commission therefore has an overview of the most important developments and decisions in the area of data protection within the EU. It has the power not only to advise Member States, the EDPB or national supervisory authorities to alter their course, it can also start legal proceedings before the Court of Justice. For example, as explained in section 6.3, Member States have been found in violation of the EU data protection framework in the past because their national legislation did not adequately guarantee the independence of the national supervisory authorities. These cases were initiated by the European Commission. Likewise, when the European Commission feels that a Member State has gone too far in limiting specific parts of the GDPR in connection with, for example, the freedom of expression, the Commission may ask the Court of Justice to assess the validity of the national law.

13. By 25 May 2020 and every four years thereafter, the Commission should submit a report on the evaluation and review of the GDPR to the European Parliament and to the Council, in which it pays particular attention to the transfer of personal data to third countries, the cooperation between national supervisory authorities and the consistency of the actions taken by them. For this task, the Commission may request information from Member States and supervisory authorities.

14. The Commission has the authority to propose amendments to the GDPR, in particular taking into account developments in information technology and the information society.
15. The Commission also has the authority to propose amendments to other EU legislation in the field of, or having an effect on, the protection of personal data, to ensure uniform and consistent protection of natural persons, in particular with respect to processing activities by EU institutions.

6.7   Implementing acts

As explained in Chapter 1, one of the reasons for adopting the GDPR was that EU Member States differed as to the ways in which they implemented the rules of the 1995 Directive in their national legislation. This led to legal uncertainties for companies and citizens. For that reason, there is now a Regulation instead of a Directive, as a Regulation has 'direct effect', meaning that citizens can invoke the Regulation directly. However, there are a small number of points on which the GDPR allows Member States to adopt their own rules. The most important are:

1. The age at which parental consent is required for processing the data of minors, within the limits set by the GDPR (section 3.3);
2. The extent to which civil society organisations can engage in representative or collective actions or in public interest litigation (section 5.10);
3. The extent to which and the conditions under which it is permitted to process sensitive personal data (section 3.4);
4. The conditions under which exceptions can be made to specific parts of the GDPR (section 2.4):
   a. Member States may adopt laws in which they limit the data subject's rights (Chapter 5) and the duty of organisations to inform the data subject of any data leak (section 4.10) when data processing is in the public interest.

This can be necessary in the light of national security or public order, important economic or financial interests, or guaranteeing the independence of the judiciary or guaranteeing the rights and interests of citizens; or

b. Member States may adopt laws in which they limit the data protection principles for certain contexts through a national law, when this is deemed necessary for freedom of expression and information, providing public access to official documents, maintaining a national identification number, employment law, archiving or statistical, scientific or historical research, guaranteeing professional secrecy or allowing churches and religious associations to process personal data in the course of their activities.

These national laws will not be discussed in detail here, as they differ from country to country, but for organisations doing business in, say, Luxembourg, Ireland and Cyprus, it is essential to critically assess and comply with the laws implementing the GDPR in these three countries.

6.8   Court judgments

Finally, it is important to be aware of and to abide by the judgments of courts. Courts have the ultimate power over the correct interpretation of the data protection framework. Most cases will be dealt with by national courts (court of first instance, court of appeal, supreme court), but cases can also go to European courts. European courts are higher than national courts, and national courts should abide by and respect the decisions of these courts. When a citizen or an organisation disagrees with a verdict of the national court, she can go to a European court to challenge that decision.

There are two European courts.

The Court of Justice is the court of the European Union, overseeing the interpretation of all EU laws and legal documents. It can invalidate national implementations of EU instruments, it can annul decisions by national courts and it can even strike down EU instruments, such as directives and regulations, for example if it feels that the EU legislator has violated one of the fundamental rights contained in the Charter of Fundamental Rights. Consequently, the Court of Justice has authority to assess the interpretation and application of the General Data Protection Regulation, and it will do so in the light of Article 8 of the Charter of Fundamental Rights of the European Union, containing the fundamental right to data protection.

The European Court of Human Rights (ECtHR) is a body of the Council of Europe. Consequently, it does not oversee EU legislation such as the GDPR; it has ultimate authority over the interpretation and application of the European Convention on Human Rights, which in Article 8 contains the right to privacy. Although the Convention, adopted in 1950, does not contain an independent right to data protection, the ECtHR acknowledges and provides protection to most important data protection principles by referring to the right to privacy. The European Court of Human Rights is the leading court in the field of privacy and data protection, and is often quoted and followed by the Court of Justice.

The Charter of Fundamental Rights explicitly states that the interpretation of the rights enshrined in the European Convention on Human Rights must be considered by the Court of Justice, and there were plans, though interestingly these were struck down by the Court of Justice, to have the EU itself (and thus not only its Member States) accede to the European Convention on Human Rights. Although there is no official hierarchy between the two courts, unofficially the European Court of Human Rights has priority over and will be followed by the European Court of Justice.

6.9 Sanctions imposed by the national supervisory authority

If you fail to comply with the rules of the GDPR, the Implementing Act, the guidelines of the national supervisory authority, the lead supervisory authority, the European Data Protection Board or the European Commission, or any other relevant legislation, two things can happen: supervisory authorities can impose sanctions (discussed in this section) and courts can impose sanctions (section 6.10).

As discussed in section 6.3, supervisory authorities have various tools at their disposal. These will usually be implemented following an escalation ladder. First, the supervisory authority will typically advise an organisation on how to process personal data in a GDPR-compliant manner; then the supervisory authority can issue a warning; subsequently it can give specific instructions; if the instructions are ignored, it can order an organisation to stop processing personal data; and only if the organisation continues to ignore the instructions will the supervisory authority impose a fine. Obviously, the authority is authorised to impose a fine right away, but it will typically only do so in matters of negligence and with respect to large organisations that structurally ignore the data protection principles.

As regards imposing an administrative fine, the supervisory authority will typically also use an escalation ladder. A small violation of the GDPR by a first-time offender will usually not lead to a heavy fine. The GDPR specifies several principles that supervisory authorities should take into account when determining the amount of an administrative fine:

1. the nature, gravity and duration of the infringement;
2. the nature, scope or purpose of the processing concerned;
3. the number of data subjects affected;
4. the level of damage suffered by them;
5. the intentional or negligent character of the infringement;
6. any action taken by the controller or processor to mitigate the damage suffered by data subjects;
7. the degree of responsibility of the controller or processor taking into account technical and organisational measures implemented;
8. any relevant previous infringements by the controller or processor;

9. the degree of cooperation with the supervisory authority, in order to remedy the infringement and mitigate the possible adverse effects of the infringement;
10. the categories of personal data affected by the infringement;
11. whether, and if so to what extent, the controller or processor brought the infringement to the attention of the supervisory authority;
12. whether the data controller or processor have ignored previous instructions by the supervisory authority;
13. whether the data controller or processor have adhered to approved codes of conduct or certification mechanisms;
14. any other aggravating or mitigating factor applicable to the circumstances of the case, such as financial benefits gained, or losses avoided, directly or indirectly, from the infringement.

6.10   Sanctions imposed by a court

In the event of an alleged violation of the GDPR by an organisation, the data subject is free to go either to the supervisory authority or to court, or both, for redress.

The data subject can lodge a complaint with the court if she disagrees with a decision taken by the national supervisory authority, for example because the authority has not found a violation of the GDPR, while the data subject believes there is one, or because the data subject had expected a higher sanction to be imposed on a data controller or processor.

The data subject can also go to court to seek compensation for damage suffered due to a GDPR violation by a data controller or processor; a court may provide financial remuneration and can adopt alternative measures, such as ordering an organisation to stop processing personal data or to organise its processes differently. In general, it can take any measure that the supervisory authority can adopt.

As explained in sections 5.10 and 6.7, if a Member State so decides, a data subject can be assisted or represented by not-for-profit civil rights organisations. Such procedures may either take the form of an opt-in or an opt-out mechanism, depending on Member State law. Member States can also allow such organisations to start procedures in the public interest.

Data controllers and processors can also go to court, for example when they collaborate with multiple parties and one organisation has not complied with their contractual agreements with respect to the protection of personal data. A controller or processor can also go to court because it disagrees with a decision taken by a national supervisory authority or the EDPB. For example, if the supervisory authority decides to impose an administrative fine or otherwise sanction an organisation, that organisation may challenge the decisions before the court. It is the court that has the ultimate say in such disputes.

If a data subject holds one or more organisations liable for damage suffered, the GDPR states that the data subject can claim for both material damage (for example, the costs of removing leaked data) and immaterial damage (for example, financial compensation for the fact that sensitive data have become public). In principle, the data controller is liable for any damages; the processor is only liable for damages to the extent that they result from its own actions and that it has not respected either the obligations the GDPR imposes on processors or the obligations the data controller and the processor had agreed upon and that are laid down in their contractual arrangement (section 2.5).

If several controllers or processors are involved in processing personal data and are responsible for the damage following from a GDPR violation, each party can be held liable for the full amount. In case of shared responsibility for the GDPR violation, the organisation that has been held liable for the full amount can subsequently recover part of those damages from the organisations sharing responsibility. This provision ensures that the data subject can file a complaint against one party, which has sufficient resources; it is not up to her to find out exactly which organisation was responsible for what part of the violation. She can simply hold one party liable.

Just like with respect to consent, the GDPR provides for a reversal of the burden of proof in relation to damages. In principle, if damage is caused by non-compliant data processing, the organisation processing the data is liable. Only if the controller or processor can demonstrate and prove that it was in no way responsible for the matter causing the damage can it avoid liability.

Finally, the national supervisory authority has the power to bring infringements of the GDPR to the attention of the judicial authorities and to start legal proceedings in order to enforce the provisions of the GDPR.

6.11   Conclusion

This last chapter discussed how the GDPR is applied in practice, which additional guidelines and codes can be adopted and how potential violations of the data protection framework are monitored and sanctioned.

First, the GDPR allows organisations to draw up codes of conduct, through which a sector agrees on a specific implementation and interpretation of the data protection framework. Drawing up such a code is not mandatory, but when a branch organisation or representative body has adopted a code of conduct, all its members must adhere to it. Second, the GDPR allows certification bodies to issue certificates, through which an organisation can show that it is GDPR-compliant with respect to, for example, taking adequate technical and organisational security measures. The national supervisory authority, or the EDPB when EU-wide codes or certificates are involved, has the power to approve codes and certifying bodies and to monitor how these self-regulatory instruments are applied in practice.

In addition, the GDPR grants the national supervisory authority, the lead supervisory authority, the European Data Protection Board and the European Commission powers to issue further rules and guidelines on the correct interpretation and implementation of the data protection framework in practice. They also have powers to take appropriate measures when a violation of the GDPR is established.

Although in general, the GDPR has direct effect, it allows Member States to adopt specific rules on four aspects of the data protection framework in particular: the age at which parental consent is required for processing the data of minors; to what extent civil society organisations can engage in representative or collective actions; to what extent and under which conditions it is permitted to process sensitive personal data; and under which conditions specific exceptions to the GDPR can be made for reasons of public interest. Consequently, organisations must also take into account the national implementation laws of the Member States they have an establishment in or about whose citizens they process personal data. A final source of data protection rules are the judgments of the courts – the national courts of Member States, the European Court of Justice and the European Court of Human Rights. They may provide further guidance on the privacy and data protection principles that must be taken into account in specific situations.

If an organisation does not comply with the data protection framework, either a supervisory authority can impose sanctions and fines or courts can impose sanctions and award damages.

7. Summary of recitals and articles per section

7.1 Chapter 1

Recitals	Articles
	Article 1 § 1 (the GDPR lays down rules for the protection of data subjects and of the free movement of personal data)
	Article 1 § 2 (the GDPR protects the rights and interests of data subjects)
	Article 1 § 3 (the GDPR protects the free movement of personal data within the EU)
Recital 12 (the GDPR is based on Article 16 of the Treaty on the Functioning of the EU)	
Recital 171 (explanation of Article 94)	Article 94 (Data Protection Directive 1995 is revoked)
Recital 172 (European Data Protection Supervisor has been consulted)	Article 99 (GDPR applies as of 25 May 2018)

	Recitals	Articles
Personal data (section 2.1)	Recital 14 (GDPR applies to processing personal data of natural persons, not of legal persons)	Article 4 § 1 (definition of personal data)
	Recital 26 (GDPR does not apply to anonymised data)	
	Recital 27 (GDPR does not apply to processing personal data about deceased persons)	
	Recital 28 (pseudonymising personal data is laudable)	Article 4 § 5 (definition of pseudonymisation)
	Recital 29 (further details about pseudonymisation)	
	Recital 30 (identification is possible via IP addresses, cookies and similar tools)	
Processing (section 2.2)	Recital 15 (provides further guidance on Article 2 § 1)	Article 2 § 1 (GDPR applies to automated processing and to manual processing if the data are contained in a filing system)
		Article 4 § 2 (definition of processing)
		Article 4 § 6 (definition of filing system)
EU regulatory competence (section 2.3)	Recital 2 (the GDPR applies to all natural persons within the EU, whatever their nationality or residence)	
	Recital 22 (when Article 3 § 1 applies, it is irrelevant whether the personal data are processed on EU soil)	Article 3 § 1 (GDPR applies to processing of personal data in the context of the activities of an establishment of a controller or a processor in the EU)
	Recital 23 (provides further guidance on what are considered goods and services in the sense of Article 3 § 2 sub a)	Article 3 § 2 (GDPR is also applicable to organisations that do not have an establishment in the EU, when they (a) offer goods and services to data subjects in the EU or (b) monitor their behaviour)
	Recital 24 (provides further guidance on what is considered monitoring in the sense of Article 3 § 2 sub b)	
	Recital 25 (provides further guidance on the applicability of Article 3 § 3)	Article 3 § 3 (GDPR is also applicable to a controller not established in the Union, but in a place where Member State law applies by virtue of public international law)
		Article 4 § 17 (definition of representative)
	Recital 80 (provides further guidance on Article 27)	Article 27 § 1 (organisation must appoint a representative when Article 3 § 2 applies)

	Recitals	Articles
		Article 27 § 2 (unless it regards (a) occasional and low risk processing of non-sensitive data or (b) processing by a public authority or body)
		Article 27 § 3 (representative should be established in one of the Member States where the relevant data subjects live)
		Article 27 § 4 (representative is point of contact for data subjects and supervisory authorities)
		Article 27 § 5 (appointing a representative does not mean that the controller or processor cannot be subject to legal action)
Exceptions (section 2.4)	Recital 16 (provides further guidance on exceptions contained in Article 2 § 2 sub a and b)	Article 2 § 2 (GDPR is not applicable to (a) matters of national security, (b) matters of common foreign policy, (c) processing of personal data by natural persons for personal reasons, or (d) processing of personal data for law enforcement purposes)
	Recital 18 (provides further guidance on the exception contained in Article 2 § 2 sub c)	
	Recital 19 (provides further guidance on the exception contained in Article 2 § 2 sub d)	
	Recital 17 (a separate data protection framework applies to EU institutions)	Article 2 § 3 (GDPR does not apply to EU institutions processing personal data)
	Recital 21 (provides further guidance on Article 2 § 4)	Article 2 § 4 (GDPR does not affect the rules on the liability of internet intermediaries contained in the e-Commerce Directive)
	Recital 73 (provides further guidance on Article 23)	Article 23 (Member States may limit the rights of data subjects when provided by law and in the public interest)
	Recital 153 (provides further guidance on Article 85)	Article 85 (Member States can restrict the applicability of specific parts of the GDPR through national law when necessary in light of freedom of expression)
	Recital 154 (provides further guidance on Article 86)	Article 86 (Member States can restrict the applicability of specific parts of the GDPR through national law when necessary in light of open access to public documents)
		Article 87 (Member States can restrict the applicability of specific parts of the GDPR through national law when necessary for maintaining a national identification number)

	Recitals	Articles
	Recital 155 (provides further guidance on Article 88)	Article 88 (Member States can restrict the applicability of specific parts of the GDPR through national law when necessary in the context of employment)
	Recital 156 (provides further guidance on the restrictions to the GDPR that can be laid down in light of Article 89)	Article 89 (Member States can restrict the applicability of specific parts of the GDPR through national law when necessary for scientific or historic research, archiving or statistical research)
	Recital 157 (importance of coupling data for scientific research)	
	Recital 158 (importance of archiving in the public interest; the GDPR does not apply to data about deceased persons)	
	Recital 159 (gives further guidance on data processing for scientific research)	
	Recital 160 (gives further guidance on data processing for historical research)	
	Recital 162 (gives further guidance on data processing for statistical purposes)	
	Recital 163 (statistical principles should be respected)	
	Recital 164 (provides further guidance on Article 90)	Article 90 (Member States can restrict the applicability of specific parts of the GDPR through national law when necessary to uphold obligations of professional secrecy)
	Recital 165 (provides further guidance on Article 91)	Article 91 (Member States can leave intact specific rules for processing personal data by churches and religious institutions established prior to the GDPR, as long as they are brought into conformity with the GDPR)
	Recital 173 (provides further guidance on Article 95)	Article 95 (when the e-Privacy Directive provides rules on points also covered by the GDPR, the e-Privacy Directive has priority)
Data controller (section 2.5)		Article 4 § 7 (definition of controller)
		Article 4 § 8 (definition of processor)
	Recital 79 (provides further guidance on Article 26 § 1)	Article 26 § 1 (when there is more than one data controller, they have to lay down the division of responsibilities in an agreement)
		Article 26 § 2 (the essence of such an agreement is available to the relevant data subjects)

Recitals	Articles
	Article 26 § 3 (the data subject can always invoke her rights vis-à-vis any of the joint controllers)
Recital 81 (provides further guidance on Article 26 § 1)	Article 28 § 1 (a controller may only contract a processor when the latter has taken adequate technical and organisational measures to be GDPR-compliant)
	Article 28 § 2 (processor only contracts a sub-processor with the permission of the controller)
	Article 28 § 3 (controller and processor should lay down the division of responsibilities in a contract)
	Article 28 § 4 (such an agreement shall extend to the sub-processor contracted by the processor)
	Article 28 § 5 (adherence to a code of conduct or certification mechanism can help a processor to demonstrate that sufficient guarantees have been taken)
	Article 28 § 6 (the contracts referred to in paragraphs 3 and 4 can be based on standard contractual clauses)
	Article 28 § 7 (the Commission may lay down standard contractual clauses for the legal relationship between the controller and processor, and the processor and sub-processor)
	Article 28 § 8 (the supervisory authority may lay down standard contractual clauses for the legal relationship between the controller and processor, and the processor and sub-processor)
	Article 28 § 9 (the contracts referred to in paragraphs 3 and 4 shall be concluded in written, electronic form)
	Article 28 § 10 (if a party has been contracted to be a processor, but subsequently processes the personal data for its own purposes, it shall be deemed to be the controller)
	Article 29 (processing activities take place on the initiative of the controller alone)

	Recitals	Articles
Necessity, proportionality, subsidiarity and effectiveness (section 3.1)	Recital 1 (the right to data protection is a fundamental right)	
	Recital 4 (underlines the principle of proportionality)	
Fair Information Principles (section 3.2)	Recital 39 (provides further guidance on the FIPs)	Article 5 § 1 sub a (lays down the principles of legitimacy, fairness and transparency)
	Recital 50 (provides further guidance on the purpose limitation principle)	Article 5 § 1 sub b (lays down the principles of purpose specification and limitation)
		Article 6 § 4 (provides further guidance on the purpose limitation principle)
		Article 5 § 1 sub c (lays down the principle of data minimisation)
		Article 5 § 1 sub d (lays down the principle of accuracy)
		Article 5 § 1 sub e (lays down the storage limitation principle)
		Article 5 § 1 sub f (lays down the principle of technical and organisational security)
		Article 5 § 2 (the controller is responsible for upholding the FIPs)
Legitimate processing of personal data (section 3.3)	Recital 40 (a controller should have a legitimate ground for processing personal data)	
	Recital 32 (provides further guidance on consent)	Article 4 § 11 (definition of consent)
	Recital 33 (consent for scientific research)	Article 6 § 1 sub a (contains the first legitimate ground for processing personal data: consent given by the data subject)
	Recital 42 (consent should be demonstrable, clear and specific)	Article 7 § 1 (burden of proof lies on controller with respect to demonstrating the legitimacy of obtained consent)
		Article 7 § 2 (when there are different purposes or matters covered by an agreement, consent must be obtained separately for each purpose or matter)

Recitals	Articles
	Article 7 § 3 (data subject can always withdraw her consent)
Recital 43 (consent should be freely given)	Article 7 § 4 (provides further guidance on what it means to give consent freely)
Recital 38 (children should be protected, especially online)	Article 4 § 25 (definition of information society services, i.e. online service providers)
	Article 8 § 1 (for information society services, children aged at least 16 years can give legitimate consent, children younger than 13 years cannot)
	Article 8 § 2 (if children cannot give legitimate consent, parental consent is required)
	Article 8 § 3 (the GDPR does not affect the general requirements of contract law)
Recital 44 (provides further guidance on Article 6 § 1 sub b)	Article 6 § 1 sub b (contains the second legitimate ground for processing personal data: processing is necessary for the performance of a contract to which the data subject is party or in order to take steps at the request of the data subject prior to entering into a contract)
Recital 46 (the vital interest of the data subject or another natural person can only be invoked if no other legitimate ground for processing applies)	Article 6 § 1 sub d (contains the third legitimate ground for processing personal data: processing is necessary in order to protect the vital interests of the data subject or of another natural person)
Recital 45 (provides further guidance on article 6 § 1 sub c and e)	Article 6 § 1 sub c (contains the fourth legitimate ground for processing personal data: processing is necessary for compliance with a legal obligation to which the controller is subject)
Recital 41 (the legal basis or legislative measure should be laid down in a clear and precise manner)	Article 6 § 1 sub e (contains the fifth legitimate ground for processing personal data: processing is necessary for the performance of a task carried out in the public interest or to exercise official authority vested in the controller)
	Article 6 § 2 (Member States may lay down further requirements for data processing based on Article 6 § 1 sub c and e)
	Article 6 § 3 (processing based on Article 6 § 1 sub c and e should be laid down in an EU or Member State law)

	Recitals	Articles
	Recital 47 (provides further guidance on Article 6 § 1 sub f)	Article 6 § 1 sub f (contains the sixth legitimate ground for processing personal data: processing is necessary for the legitimate interests pursued by the controller or by a third party, except where such interests are overridden by the interests or fundamental rights and freedoms of the data subject)
	Recital 48 (a legitimate interest can be transferring personal data within the different establishments of one organisation)	Article 4 § 10 (definition of third party)
	Recital 49 (a legitimate interest can be processing personal data for information security reasons)	
Legitimate processing of sensitive personal data (section 3.4)	Recital 34 (provides further guidance on genetic data)	Article 4 § 13 (definition of genetic data)
		Article 4 § 14 (definition of biometric data)
	Recital 35 (provides further guidance on health data)	Article 4 § 15 (definition of health data)
	Recital 51 (provides further guidance on the extent to which photos should by definition be considered to contain sensitive personal data, such as racial data)	Article 9 § 1 (processing sensitive personal data is prohibited, where sensitive data are personal data revealing racial or ethnic origin, political opinions, religious or philosophical beliefs, or trade union membership, and the processing of genetic data, biometric data for the purpose of uniquely identifying a natural person, data concerning health or data concerning a natural person's sex life or sexual orientation)
	Recital 52 (processing sensitive data is allowed when in the public interest)	Article 9 § 2 (unless processing is based on (a) explicit consent, (b) employment and social security law, (c) vital interests of data subject, or (d) processing activities are performed by unions, churches or political organisations, (e) the data subject has manifestly made the data public, (f) processing is necessary for a legal claim, (g) for a substantial public interest, (h) for occupational medicine, (i) public health, or (j) archiving, scientific or historical research or statistics).
	Recital 53 (processing sensitive data is allowed for health-related purposes)	Article 9 § 3 (exception article 9 § 2 sub h only applies when sensitive data are processed by a person bound by professional secrecy)

	Recitals	Articles
	Recital 54 (when necessary for health-related purposes)	Article 9 § 4 (Member States may lay down additional requirements with respect to processing genetic, biometric and health data)
	Recital 55 (religious organisations may need to process sensitive data)	
	Recital 56 (political organisations may need to process the political opinions of their members)	
	Recital 161 (there are specific requirements with respect to consent for clinical trials)	
		Article 10 (specifies the rules for processing personal data relating to criminal convictions and offences or related security measures)
Legitimate transfer of personal data to non-EU countries (section 3.5)	Recital 5 (cross-border data processing within the EU has increased)	
	Recital 6 (cross-border data processing with organisations in non-EU countries has increased)	
	Recital 7 (that is why it is important to have a strong and coherent data protection regime)	
	Recital 8 (to the extent that the GDPR leaves room for Member States to interpret the rules, they should do so in a way promoting the coherence and comprehensibility of the EU data protection regime)	
	Recital 3 (the goal of the Data Protection Directive was to harmonise the rules within the EU)	
	Recital 9 (despite these efforts, data protection rules within the EU were fragmented)	
	Recital 13 (the GDPR provides more legal certainty to data subjects and organisations processing personal data)	
	Recital 10 (however, Member States are allowed to adopt sector-specific rules and regulations)	
	Recital 11 (the GDPR provides for stronger enforcement capacities)	

Recitals	Articles
Recital 31 (gives further guidance on Article 4 § 9)	Article 4 § 9 (gives the definition of recipient)
	Article 4 § 18 (gives the definition of an enterprise)
Recital 37 (gives further guidance on Article 4 § 19)	Article 4 § 19 (gives the definition of a group of undertakings)
	Article 4 § 20 (gives the definition of binding corporate rules)
	Article 4 § 26 (gives the definition of an international organisation)
Recital 101 (gives further guidance on Article 44)	Article 44 (transfer of personal data to non-EU countries or international organisations is only allowed if one of the grounds specified in the GDPR applies)
Recital 103 (gives further guidance on Article 45)	Article 45 (the first ground for legitimately transferring personal data to non-EU countries is when the European Commission has adopted an adequacy decision with respect to a non-EU country)
Recital 104 (assessment of adequacy of a non-EU country)	
Recital 105 (the Commission should take into account regional obligations)	
Recital 106 (an adequacy decision should include a mechanism for periodical review)	
Recital 107 (adequacy decision may be revoked)	
Recital 108 (provides further guidance on Article 46)	Article 46 § 1 (the second ground for legitimately transferring personal data to non-EU countries is when an EU-based and a non-EU-based organisation have entered into a legal agreement by which the non-EU-based organisation commits itself to upholding a level of data protection that is equivalent to that provided by the GDPR)
Recital 109 (provides further guidance on standard contractual clauses)	Article 46 § 2 (there are instances where such a legal agreement will be deemed appropriate without the prior approval of the supervisory authority)
	Article 46 § 3 (there are instances where such a legal agreement will be deemed appropriate only with the prior approval of the supervisory authority)

Recitals	Articles
	Article 46 § 4 (the supervisory authority shall apply the consistency mechanism with respect to § 3)
	Article 46 § 5 (data transfer based on authorisations by a Member State, supervisory authority or the Commission prior to the GDPR shall remain valid until amended, replaced or repealed)
Recital 110 (provides further guidance on Article 47)	Article 47 § 1 (appropriate safeguards can also be achieved through binding corporate rules adopted by a group of undertakings with establishments both in the EU and non-EU countries and approved by the supervisory authority)
	Article 47 § 2 (the GDPR specifies in detail which rules and points such binding corporate rules should address)
	Article 47 § 3 (the Commission may specify the format and procedures for the exchange of information between controllers, processors and supervisory authorities for binding corporate rules)
Recital 115 (provides further guidance on Article 48)	Article 48 (data controllers and processors may only transfer personal data to a non-EU-based organisation when so ordered by a foreign court or administrative body when either a Member State or the EU has an international agreement with that foreign country)
Recital 111 (provides further guidance on Article 49)	Article 49 § 1 (the third ground for legitimately transferring personal data to non-EU countries is when it concerns an occasional data transfer, which is based on either (a) explicit consent by the data subject, (b) contractual agreement with the data subject, (c) contractual agreement in the interests of the data subject, (d) substantial public interest, (e) establishment, exercise or defence of legal claims, (f) vital interest of data subject or other natural person, (g) providing a public register, or (h) the interests of the data controller prevail over the interests of the data subject)

Recitals	Articles
Recital 112 (provides further guidance on Article 49)	Article 49 § 2 (Article 49 § 1 sub g only applies to limited transfers)
Recital 113 (provides further guidance on Article 49)	Article 49 § 3 (Article 49 § 1 sub a, b and c cannot be invoked by governmental organisations)
Recital 114 (data subjects should be granted enforceable and effective rights)	Article 49 § 4 (Article 49 § 1 sub d should be established by law)
	Article 49 § 5 (Member States may lay down restrictions for Article 49 § 1 sub d)
	Article 49 § 6 (when a controller relies on Article 49 § 1 sub h, it should document this in its register)
Recital 102 (Member States may conclude international agreements which involve the transfer of personal data to third countries or international organisations, as far as such agreements do not affect the GDPR and include an appropriate level of protection for the fundamental rights of the data subjects)	Article 96 (international agreements by Member States for transferring personal data to non-EU countries that have been established prior to the GDPR will keep their validity until amended, replaced or revoked)

	Recitals	Articles
		Article 31 (data controllers, processors and representatives should cooperate with supervisory authorities)
Documentation (section 4.1)	Recital 82 (provides further guidance on Article 30)	Article 30 § 1 (the controller should document which data it processes, how and why)
		Article 30 § 2 (the processor should document which data it processes, how and why)
		Article 30 § 3 (the register should be written and available in electronic form)
		Article 30 § 4 (the supervisory authority has access to the register upon request)
	Recital 13 (provides further guidance on Article 30 § 5)	Article 30 § 5 (exception for small organisations that occasionally process non-sensitive data)
Data Protection Policy (section 4.2)	Recital 74 (provides further guidance on Article 24)	Article 24 § 1 (the data controller should adopt adequate technical and organisational measures to ensure compliance with the GDPR)
	Recital 75 (provides further guidance on what is to be considered a risk)	
	Recital 76 (risks should be determined with reference to the nature, scope, context and purposes of the processing)	
	Recital 78 (provides further guidance on Article 24 § 2)	Article 24 § 2 (the data controller should adopt internal data protection policies proportionate to its processing activities)
	Recital 77 (provides further guidance on Article 24 § 3)	Article 24 § 3 (codes of conduct and certification mechanisms can help with ensuring compliance with the GDPR)
Data Protection by design and by default (section 4.3)	Recital 78 (provides further guidance on Article 25)	Article 25 § 1 (the data controller should implement policy choices by design in its technical infrastructure)
		Article 25 § 2 (the data controller should implement policy choices by default in its technical infrastructure)

	Recitals	Articles
		Article 25 § 3 (an approved certification mechanism may be used as an element to demonstrate compliance with the requirement to implement policy choices by design and by default)
Informing the general public (section 4.4)	Recital 58 (providing information via a website is of particular relevance in situations where the proliferation of actors and the technological complexity of practice make it difficult for the data subject to know and understand whether, by whom and for what purpose personal data relating to him or her are being collected, such as in the case of online advertising. Information communication to children should be in plain and simple language)	
		Article 14 § 5 sub b (an exception to the duty of the controller to inform the data subject about the data it processes about her, why and how applies when the provision of such information proves impossible or would involve a disproportionate effort. In such a case, the controller should take appropriate measures to protect the data subject's rights and freedoms and legitimate interests, including making the information publicly available)
		Article 34 § 3 sub c (an exception to the duty to inform data subjects of a data breach with a high impact on their interests applies when this would involve disproportionate effort. In such a case, there shall instead be a public communication or a similar measure whereby the data subjects are informed in an equally effective manner)
Informing the data subject (section 4.5)	Recital 60 (provides further guidance on Articles 13 and 14)	Article 13 § 1 and 2 (when the data controller has obtained personal data from the data subject directly, it should immediately inform the data subject that it processes personal data about her, which data it processes, how and why)
	Recital 61 (provides further guidance on the terms in Articles 13 and 14)	Article 13 § 3 (the data controller should inform the data subject of the fact that it intends to process her personal data for new purposes)

Recitals	Articles
Recital 62 (provides further guidance on the exceptions to Articles 13 and 14)	Article 13 § 4 (information duty of paragraphs 1, 2 and 3 do not apply when the data subject already has the information)
	Article 14 § 1 and 2 (if the data controller has not obtained personal data directly from the data subject, it should also inform the data subject of the fact that it processes personal data about her, which data it processes, why and how, in addition to information about the source of the data)
	Article 14 § 3 (time frame for providing such information)
	Article 14 § 4 (the data controller should inform the data subject of the fact that it intends to process her personal data for new purposes)
	Article 14 § 5 (specifies four situations in which the information duty of paragraphs 1, 2 and 4 does not apply)
	Article 12 § 7 (the data controller may provide the data subject with information using icons)
	Article 12 § 8 (Commission may adopt rules on icons)
Data Protection Impact Assessment (section 4.6)	Recital 89 (under the Data Protection Directive, the supervisory authority was authorised to do impact assessments, but this resulted in high administrative burdens)	Article 4 § 4 (definition of profiling)
	Recital 90 (provides further guidance on the obligation to do an impact assessment)	
	Recital 84 (provides further guidance on Article 35)	Article 35 § 1 (the data controller has to perform an impact assessment when an intended processing activity entails a high risk for data subjects)
	Recital 95 (the processor should assist the data controller when executing the impact assessment)	Article 35 § 2 (where a controller has appointed a data protection officer, the officer should be involved)
	Recital 91 (provides further guidance on Article 35 § 3)	Article 35 § 3 (an impact assessment is required with respect to (a) extensive evaluation of personal aspects of data subjects based on automated decision-making and profiling, (b) processing sensitive personal data on a large scale, and (c) systematic monitoring of a publicly accessible area on a large scale)

Recitals	Articles
	Article 35 § 4 (the supervisory authority can adopt a list of operations for which a DPIA is required)
	Article 35 § 5 (the supervisory authority can adopt a list of operations for which no DPIA is required)
	Article 35 § 6 (in case of § 4 or 5, the consistency mechanism applies)
Recital 92 (there are circumstances under which it may be reasonable and economical for the subject of a data protection impact assessment to be broader than a single project)	Article 35 § 7 (provides further guidance on the content of the impact assessment)
	Article 35 § 8 (when assessing the risk, where applicable, the code of conduct shall be taken into account)
	Article 35 § 9 (where appropriate, the controller shall seek the views of data subjects or their representatives)
Recital 93 (impact assessment can be done before adopting a law)	Article 35 § 10 (the data controller does not have to perform a DPIA when processing is based on a legal obligation or public interest (section 3.3) and a general DPIA was conducted in the course of adopting the EU or Member State law which contains the legal obligation or public interest)
	Article 35 § 11 (the controller shall carry out a review to assess whether processing is performed in accordance with the data protection impact assessment at least when there is a change in the risk represented by processing operations)
Recital 94 (provides further guidance on Article 36 § 1)	Article 36 § 1 (when the DPIA indicates that a data processing initiative involves a high risk, the controller should consult with the supervisory authority before processing the data)
	Article 36 § 2 (the supervisory authority advises on whether or not to continue the project and on the potential conditions)
	Article 36 § 3 (the controller should provide the supervisory authority with all relevant information)

	Recitals	Articles
	Recital 96 (provides further guidance on Article 36 § 4)	Article 36 § 4 (the supervisory authority should be consulted when adopting a law which entails processing personal data)
		Article 36 § 5 (Member States may adopt legal provisions specifying other situations in which controllers should consult the supervisory authority before starting a data processing initiative, where processing is based on a public interest or task or the interest of public health)
Data Protection Officer (section 4.7)	Recital 97 (provides further guidance on Article 37)	Article 37 § 1 (controllers and processors should appoint a data protection officer when (a) a governmental organisation is concerned, (b) data processing entails regular and systematic monitoring of data subjects on a large scale, or (c) data processing entails processing sensitive personal data on a large scale)
		Article 37 § 2 (a group of undertakings may appoint a single data protection officer)
		Article 37 § 3 (governmental organisations may share a data protection officer)
		Article 37 § 4 (EU or Member State law may stipulate additional situations in which a controller or processor needs to appoint a data protection officer)
		Article 37 § 5 (the officer should be skilled and competent)
		Article 37 § 6 (the officer is a staff member or has a service contract)
		Article 37 § 7 (the contact details of the officer should be made public)
		Article 38 § 1 (involvement of officer)
		Article 38 § 2 (access to information by officer)
		Article 38 § 3 (independence of officer)
		Article 38 § 4 (officer is contact point for data subjects)
		Article 38 § 5 (officer is bound by professional secrecy)

	Recitals	Articles
		Article 38 § 6 (an officer may perform other functions, as long as there is no conflict of interest)
		Article 39 § 1 (the tasks of an officer are to (a) advise the organisation, (b) monitor its GDPR compliance, (c) advise on impact assessments, (d) cooperate with the supervisory authority, and (e) be the contact point for the supervisory authority)
		Article 39 § 2 (when performing her work, the officer should take account of the risks involved with data processing initiatives)
Technical and organisational security measures (sections 4.8 and 4.9)	Recital 83 (provides further guidance on Article 32)	Article 32 § 1 (the controller and processor should adopt adequate technical and organisational security measures)
		Article 32 § 2 (what is deemed adequate depends on the risks concerned)
		Article 32 § 3 (codes of conduct and certificates can help establish an adequate level of technical and organisational security)
		Article 32 § 4 (measures should also be adopted to prevent abuse by employees that have access to the data)
Data breach notification (section 4.10)	Recital 87 (all appropriate technological protection and organisational measures should be implemented to establish immediately whether a personal data breach has taken place and to inform promptly the supervisory authority and the data subject)	Article 4 § 12 (definition of personal data breach)
	Recital 85 (provides further guidance on Article 33)	Article 33 § 1 (the controller should report a data breach to the supervisory authority, unless the breach is unlikely to result in risks for data subjects)
		Article 33 § 2 (the processor should notify the controller of a breach)

Recitals	Articles
Recital 88 (provides further guidance on the format and procedures for informing the supervisory authority and the data subject)	Article 33 § 3 (the controller should provide the supervisory authority with all relevant information)
	Article 33 § 4 (the information may be provided in phases, where necessary)
	Article 33 § 5 (the controller should document the breach)
Recital 86 (provides further guidance on Article 34)	Article 34 § 1 (the data controller should report a data breach to the data subjects when there are high risks)
	Article 34 § 2 (the data subject should be given all relevant information)
	Article 34 § 3 (exception to the duty to inform data subjects when (a) adequate security measures have been taken before the data breach occurred, (b) after the data breach occurred, or (c) when this would entail a disproportionate effort)
	Article 34 § 4 (the supervisory authority can overrule a data controller relying on § 3)

	Recital	Article
	Recital 57 (provides further guidance on Article 11)	Article 11 § 1 (if the controller no longer needs personal data, it should not retain them for the sole purpose of complying with the obligations in the GDPR)
		Article 11 § 2 (when the controller has deleted personal data according to § 1 and can no longer identify a data subject, it should not fulfil requests from a data subject with respect to her rights contained in Articles 15-20, unless she provides further details to allow identification)
	Recital 59 (provides further guidance on Article 12)	Article 12 § 1 (communication with data subject should be clear and understandable; in writing, unless the data subject indicates a different preference; and preferably electronically)
		Article 12 § 2 (if the controller cannot establish the identity of a data subject, it does not have to comply with her requests)
		Article 12 § 3 (time path for communication)
		Article 12 § 4 (negative decision)
		Article 12 § 5 (communication is free of charge; when requests are clearly unfounded or excessive, a controller may refuse to comply or ask for remuneration for complying with the requests)
		Article 12 § 6 (in the case of § 2, the controller is allowed to request further details needed to establish the identity of the data subject)
Right to information (section 5.1)	Recital 63 (provides further guidance on the right to information)	Article 15 § 1 (the data subject may ask the data controller to provide information about which data are processed about her, why and how)
		Article 15 § 2 (if personal data are transferred outside the EU, the data subject may also inquire about the legal ground for the transfer of personal data)
Right to access (section 5.2)	Recital 63 (provides further guidance on the right to access, with particular attention to accessing one's medical file)	Article 15 § 1 (the data subject may request access to the personal data being processed about her)

	Recital	Article
	Recital 64 (confirms that the data controller should establish the identity of the data subject before granting access)	
Right to copy (section 5.3)		Article 15 § 3 (the data subject has a right to copy the data being processed about her)
		Article 15 § 4 (the right to copy should not undermine the rights of others)
Right to data portability (section 5.4)	Recital 68 (provides further guidance on Article 20)	Article 20 § 1 (the right to data portability applies when (a) processing is based on consent or contract and (b) processing is carried out by automated means)
		Article 20 § 2 (where possible, the data should be sent to the new data controller)
		Article 20 § 3 (the right to be forgotten continues to be applicable)
		Article 20 § 4 (the right to data portability should not undermine the rights of others)
Right to rectification and completion (section 5.5)		Article 16 (right to rectification and completion)
		Article 19 (the data controller has the obligation to inform other organisations with whom it has shared personal data that these have been corrected or completed)
Right to erasure (right to be forgotten) (section 5.6)	Recital 65 (provides further guidance on Article 17, with specific attention to the position of children)	Article 17 § 1 (data subject has the right to be forgotten when (a) the storage limitation principle has been violated, (b) and (c) the data controller has no legal grounds for processing personal data, (d) when personal data are otherwise processed unlawfully, (e) when there is a legal obligation to delete the data, or (f) when consent with respect to a minor has been withdrawn)
	Recital 66 (provides further guidance on Article 17 § 2)	Article 17 § 2 (where the controller has made public the personal data that should be deleted and these are processed by other controllers, the controller should inform them of the fact that the data should be deleted)

Recital	Article
	Article 17 § 3 (exception to the right to be forgotten when necessary in light of (a) freedom of expression, (b) compliance with a legal obligation, (c) reasons of public interest, (d) for archiving, scientific or historical research or statistical purposes, or (e) for the establishment, exercise or defence of legal claims)
	Article 19 (the data controller has the obligation to inform other organisations with whom it has shared personal data that these have been deleted)
Right not to be subject to automated decision-making (section 5.7)	Article 4 § 4 (definition of profiling)
Recital 71 (provides further guidance on Article 22, explaining when a decision has important consequences for the data subject)	Article 22 § 1 (right not to be subject to automated decision-making, including profiling, when this has important consequences for the data subject)
	Article 22 § 2 (exception for automated decision-making based on non-sensitive personal data when based on (a) a contract with the data subject, (b) a legal obligation, or (c) the explicit consent of the data subject)
	Article 22 § 3 (in case of § 2 (a) and (c), the controller should implement additional safeguards for the protection of the interests of the data subject)
	Article 22 § 4 (exception for automated decision-making based on sensitive personal data when based on (a) explicit consent or (b) substantial public interest, and the controller has implemented additional safeguards for the protection of the data subject)
Right to object (section 5.8)	Recital 69 (provides further guidance on Article 21 § 1)	Article 21 § 1 (the data subject has the right to challenge whether, in her individual case, the data controller processes personal data in the public interest or in its own interest, where the controller believes that its interests override the interests of the data subject)

	Recital	Article
	Recital 70 (provides further guidance on Article 21 § 2)	Article 21 § 2 (the data subject also has the right to object to direct marketing, which will typically be based on the interests of the data controller)
		Article 21 § 3 (requests pursuant to § 2 should be granted)
		Article 21 § 4 (the data controller should inform the data subject of her right to object)
		Article 21 § 5 (the right to object may be exercised by automated means)
		Article 21 § 6 (the right to object is also applicable to data processing in the course of archiving, scientific or historical research or statistics, unless this processing is in the public interest)
Right to restrict (section 5.9)		Article 4 § 3 (definition of restriction of processing)
	Recital 67 (provides further guidance on Article 18)	Article 18 § 1 (right to restrict applies when (a) the data subject is awaiting a decision on a request pursuant to Article 16, (b) the processing of personal data is unlawful and the data subject prefers restriction over deletion of her data, (c) the purpose for which the data were gathered has been achieved, but they are needed for a legal claim, or (d) the data subject is awaiting a decision on a request pursuant to Article 21)
		Article 18 § 2 (exception to the right to restrict in the case of (a) data subject's consent, (b) when necessary for the establishment, exercise or defence of legal claims, (c) for the protection of the rights of another natural or legal person, or (d) for reasons of important public interest)
		Article 18 § 3 (the data controller should inform a data subject when it starts processing her data again, after they have been restricted)
		Article 19 (the data controller has the obligation to inform other organisations with whom it has shared personal data that these have been restricted)
Right to file a complaint (section 5.10)	Recital 141 (right to file a complaint)	Article 77 (the data subject can file a complaint with the supervisory authority)

Recital	Article
Recital 143 (any natural or legal person can challenge a decision by the EDBP or supervisory authority before the Court of Justice)	Article 78 (the data subject, data processor, data controller and others affected may challenge a decision by the supervisory authority before a court of law)
	Article 79 (the data subject can go to court when a data controller or processor has violated the GDPR)
Recital 142 (provides further guidance on Article 80)	Article 80 (the data subject may be represented by non-profit organisations if Member States have incorporated such possibilities in their national laws)
Recital 144 (provides further guidance on Article 81)	Article 81 (if a complaint has been filed about the same matter in another Member State, the court can suspend the proceedings)
Recital 145 (freedom of choice regarding the Member State in which the complaint is filed)	
Recital 147 (general jurisdiction rules should not prejudice the application of specific rules to jurisdictional matters contained in the GDPR)	
Recital 146 (provides further guidance on Article 82)	Article 82 § 1 (the data subject has the right to receive compensation for damages)
	Article 82 § 2 (the data controller is liable, also for actions taken by the data processor, unless the latter has violated its own obligations)
	Article 82 § 3 (the data controller and processor are not liable for damages when they are not in any way responsible for the event giving rise to the damage)
	Article 82 § 4 (if multiple organisations share responsibility, the data subject can hold any of them fully liable for all damages)
	Article 82 § 5 (the organisation that bears all damages can claim back part of the damages from the other organisations involved)
	Article 82 § 6 (competent courts can award damages)

	Recitals	Articles
Codes of conduct (section 6.1)	Recital 98 (encourages codes of conduct)	Article 40 § 1 (official institutions should promote drafting of codes of conduct)
	Recital 99 (parties concerned should be consulted)	Article 40 § 2 (representative bodies can adopt a code of conduct)
		Article 40 § 3 (codes of conduct can also apply to organisations that are not subject to the GDPR, when the Commission has approved of the code, and can lay down appropriate safeguards for transferring personal data)
		Article 40 § 4 (codes can install a body tasked with overseeing and enforcing the code)
		Article 40 § 5 (codes should be approved by the supervisory authority)
		Article 40 § 6 (the supervisory authority makes adopted codes of conduct public)
		Article 40 § 7 (EDPB can adopt an opinion on international codes of conduct)
		Article 40 § 8 (when the EDPB has issued an opinion on the validity of an international code of conduct, it has to send its opinion to the Commission)
		Article 40 § 9 (the Commission can approve an international code of conduct)
		Article 40 § 10 (the Commission publishes approved codes of conduct)
		Article 40 § 11 (EDPB shall collate all approved codes of conduct in a publicly available register)
		Article 41 § 1 (codes can install a body tasked with overseeing and enforcing the code, which does not have an effect on the powers and competences of the supervisory authority)
		Article 41 § 2 (such a body may be accredited by the supervisory authority if (a) it is competent, (b) it adequately monitors the code, (c) it adequately handles complaints, and (d) there is no conflict of interest)

	Recitals	Articles
		Article 41 § 3 (when the supervisory authority sets out criteria for § 2, it should submit them to the EDPB)
		Article 41 § 4 (an accredited body may impose sanctions when the code is violated)
		Article 41 § 5 (accreditation can be revoked)
		Article 41 § 6 (no accredited body can be installed with respect to codes applicable to governmental organisations)
Certification (section 6.2)	Recital 100 (encourages certification mechanisms)	Article 42 § 1 (official institutions should promote certification mechanisms)
		Article 42 § 2 (certificates can also apply to organisations that are not subject to the GDPR in order to demonstrate adequate safeguards being in place for the transfer of personal data)
		Article 42 § 3 (obtaining a certificate is voluntary)
		Article 42 § 4 (certification does not affect the obligations in the GDPR)
		Article 42 § 5 (certificates can be issued by a certification body or a supervisory authority on the basis of criteria adopted by the supervisory authority or the EDPB)
		Article 42 § 6 (organisations that want to apply for a certificate should provide all relevant information)
		Article 42 § 7 (duration of certificate)
		Article 42 § 8 (EDPB shall collate all approved certification mechanisms in a publicly available register)
		Article 43 § 1 (a certification body can be accredited by the supervisory authority or the national accreditation body)
		Article 43 § 2 (the conditions for accreditation of a certification body are (a) independence, (b) adherence to the criteria set out pursuant to Article 42 § 5, (c) procedures for reviewing and withdrawing certificates, (d) procedures for handling complaints, and (e) no conflict of interest)

	Recitals	Articles
		Article 43 § 3 (accreditation is performed on the basis of criteria established by national supervisory authority or EDPB)
		Article 43 § 4 (certification bodies provide controllers and processors with certificates or can withdraw them upon evaluation)
		Article 43 § 5 (certification bodies should inform the supervisory authority of certificates issued or withdrawn)
		Article 43 § 6 (the criteria for accrediting a certification body are public)
		Article 43 § 7 (accreditation can be revoked)
		Article 43 § 8 (the Commission may adopt rules on certification mechanisms)
		Article 43 § 9 (the Commission may adopt rules on technical standards for certification mechanisms)
Supervisory authority (section 6.3)		Article 4 § 21 (definition of supervisory authority)
	Recital 117 (provides further guidance on Article 51)	Article 51 § 1 (each Member State shall provide for at least one independent public authority to be responsible for monitoring the application of the GDPR)
		Article 51 § 2 (national supervisory authorities shall cooperate with each other and the Commission)
	Recital 119 (provides further guidance on Article 51 § 3)	Article 51 § 3 (where more than one supervisory authority is established in a Member State, one main supervisory authority should be appointed)
		Article 51 § 4 (Member States should inform the Commission about the laws regulating the national supervisory authority)
		Article 52 § 1 (each supervisory authority shall act with complete independence in performing its tasks and exercising its powers)
		Article 52 § 2 (board members of the supervisory authority should remain free from external influence)

Recitals	Articles
	Article 52 § 3 (board members shall refrain from any action incompatible with their duties)
Recital 120 (provides further guidance on Article 52 § 4)	Article 52 § 4 (Member States should ensure that the supervisory authority has sufficient human, technical and financial resources, premises and infrastructure necessary to perform its tasks effectively)
	Article 52 § 5 (each supervisory authority chooses and has its own staff, subject to the exclusive direction of the supervisory authority)
Recital 118 (provides further guidance on Article 52 § 6)	Article 52 § 6 (financial control of the supervisory authority should not affect its independence)
Recital 121 (provides further guidance on Article 53)	Article 53 § 1 (board members of the supervisory authority can only be appointed by the parliament, government, head of state or an independent body)
	Article 53 § 2 (board members are selected on the basis of their qualifications, experience and skills)
	Article 53 § 3 (their term shall end only in case of expiry of the term of office, resignation or compulsory retirement)
	Article 53 § 4 (a board member shall be dismissed only in cases of serious misconduct or if the member no longer fulfils the conditions for its position)
	Article 54 § 1 (Member States have to lay down in a law, among others, the criteria for board members, the fixed term in office and eligibility for reappointment)
	Article 54 § 2 (board members and the staff of the supervisory authority are bound by professional secrecy)
	Article 55 § 1 (national supervisory authorities are competent for data processing on their own territory)
	Article 55 § 2 (exception to Article 56 when data processing is based on a public interest or a legal obligation)
Recital 20 (provides further guidance on Article 55 § 3)	Article 55 § 3 (supervisory authorities are not competent to oversee courts acting in their judicial capacity)

	Recitals	Articles
	Recital 132 (describes the awareness-raising activities by supervisory authorities)	Article 57 § 1 (describes the various tasks of the national supervisory authority)
		Article 57 § 2 (supervisory authorities should facilitate complaints by data subjects via electronic means)
		Article 57 § 3 (performance of its tasks is free of charge with respect to requests from data subjects and data protection officers, but not necessarily for requests from data controllers or processors)
		Article 57 § 4 (however, where requests are manifestly unfounded or excessive, the supervisory authority may charge a reasonable fee based on administrative costs, or refuse to act on the request)
		Article 58 § 1 (describes the investigative powers of national supervisory authorities)
		Article 58 § 2 (describes the corrective powers of national supervisory authorities)
		Article 58 § 3 (describes the advisory powers of national supervisory authorities)
		Article 58 § 4 (the exercise of these powers is subject to effective judicial remedy and due process)
		Article 58 § 5 (supervisory authorities have the power to go to court when the GDPR is violated)
		Article 58 § 6 (Member States may afford more powers to supervisory authorities)
		Article 59 (national supervisory authorities should publish an annual report on their activities)
Lead supervisory authority (section 6.4)	Recital 36 (provides further guidance on Article 4 § 16)	Article 4 § 16 (definition of main establishment)
		Article 4 § 22 (definition of supervisory authority concerned)
		Article 4 § 23 (definition of cross-border processing)
		Article 4 § 24 (definition of relevant and reasoned objection, meaning the objection of a supervisory authority concerned to the decision by the lead supervisory authority)

	Recitals	Articles
	Recitals 124-131 (provide further guidance on Article 56)	Article 56 (describes the competence of the lead supervisory authority)
	Recital 122 (provides further guidance on Article 55 § 2)	Article 55 § 2 (provides one of the exceptions to Article 56, namely when a complaint has been lodged with a national supervisory authority)
		Article 60 (the lead supervisory authority and the other supervisory authorities concerned should cooperate)
	Recital 133 (provides further guidance on Article 61)	Article 61 (the national supervisory authorities shall provide each other with relevant information and mutual assistance)
	Recital 134 (provides further guidance on Article 62)	Article 62 (the national supervisory authorities can engage in joint operations including joint investigations and joint enforcement measures)
	Recitals 123 & 135-136 (provide further guidance on Article 63)	Article 63 (the supervisory authorities shall cooperate with each other and, where relevant, with the Commission)
EDPB (section 6.5)	Recital 72 (the EDPB can establish rules on profiling)	Article 64 (the EDPB can issue an opinion when a national supervisory authority adopts decisions in a number of areas, such as approval of binding corporate rules; determines standard contractual clauses; or adopts criteria for performing a DPIA)
		Article 65 (the EDPB can act as a dispute resolution body when different supervisory authorities have conflicting views)
	Recitals 137-138 (provide further guidance on Article 66)	Article 66 (where a supervisory authority concerned considers that there is an urgent need to act in order to protect the rights and freedoms of data subjects on a matter having a cross-border effect, it may do so and request an urgent opinion from the EDPB)
		Article 67 (the Commission may specify the arrangements for the exchange of information by electronic means between supervisory authorities, and between supervisory authorities and the EDPB)
		Article 68 (describes the composition of the EDPB)
	Recital 139 (provides further guidance on Article 69)	Article 69 (underlines the independence of the EDPB)

	Recitals	Articles
		Article 70 (provides the tasks of the EDPB)
		Article 71 (the EDPB has to draw up an annual report)
		Article 72 (the EDPB shall take decisions by a simple majority of its members, unless provided otherwise)
		Article 73 (the EDPB shall elect a chair)
		Article 74 (the chair has a mainly procedural role)
	Recital 140 (provides further guidance on Article 75)	Article 75 (the EDPS shall provide the EDBP with a secretariat, which shall perform its tasks exclusively on the instructions of the chair)
		Article 76 (discussion within the EDPB shall remain confidential)
Commission (section 6.6)	Recital 116 (provides further guidance on Article 50)	Article 50 (the Commission and supervisory authorities shall take steps to promote international cooperation for the protection of personal data)
	Recitals 166-170 (provide further guidance on Article 92)	Article 92 (the power of the Commission provided in Article 12 § 8 and Article 43 § 8 may be revoked at any time by the European Parliament or by the Council)
		Article 93 (the Commission shall be assisted by a committee)
		Article 97 (by 25 May 2020 and every four years thereafter, the Commission shall submit a report on the evaluation and review of the GDPR; it may propose to amend the GDPR)
		Article 98 (the Commission may propose to amend other EU legal instruments having an effect on the processing of personal data)
Implementing acts (section 6.7)		–
Court judgments (section 6.8)		–
Sanctions by supervisory authorities (section 6.9)	Recital 150 (provides further guidance on Article 83)	Article 83 § 1 (each supervisory authority has the right to impose administrative fines)

Recitals	Articles
Recital 148 (in the case of a minor infringement or if the fine likely to be imposed would constitute a disproportionate burden to a natural person, a reprimand may be issued instead of a fine)	Article 83 § 2 (describes the criteria to be taken into account when determining the amount of the fine)
	Article 83 § 3 (if a controller or processor for the same or linked processing operations infringes several provisions of the GDPR, the total amount of the administrative fine shall not exceed the amount specified for the gravest infringement)
	Article 83 § 4 (describes the situations in which the maximum amount of the administrative fine that can be imposed is 10 000 000 euros, or in the case of an undertaking, up to 2% of total worldwide annual turnover of the preceding financial year, whichever is higher)
	Article 83 § 5 (describes the situations in which the maximum amount of the administrative fine that can be imposed is 20 000 000 euros, or in the case of an undertaking, up to 4% of total worldwide annual turnover of the preceding financial year, whichever is higher)
	Article 83 § 6 (the maximum fine for non-compliance with an order by a national supervisory authority exercising one of its corrective powers is also 20 000 000 euros, or in the case of an undertaking, up to 4% of total worldwide annual turnover of the preceding financial year, whichever is higher)
	Article 83 § 7 (each Member State may lay down the rules on whether and to what extent administrative fines may be imposed on public authorities and bodies established in that Member State)
	Article 83 § 8 (laying down administrative fines should be subject to effective judicial remedy and due process)

	Recitals	Articles
		Article 83 § 9 (Member States may decide not to grant the supervisory authority the power to impose fines, but rather a national court, on the initiative of the supervisory authority; those Member States have to inform the Commission about such provisions)
	Recital 151 (provides further guidance on Article 84)	Article 84 § 1 (Member States shall lay down the rules for other penalties applicable to infringements which are not subject to administrative fines)
	Recital 149 (Member States can lay down the rules on criminal penalties for infringements of the GDPR)	Article 84 § 2 (Member States have to inform the Commission about such provisions)
	Recital 152 (Member States should implement a system which provides for effective, proportionate and dissuasive penalties)	
Sanctions by courts (section 6.10)		–